NOTES ON THE LANDSCAPE OF HOME

SUSAN HAND SHETTERLY

Down East Books

CAMDEN, MAINE

Down East Books

An imprint of Globe Pequot, the trade division of The Rowman & Littlefield
Publishing Group, Inc.
4501 Forbes Blvd., Ste. 200
Lanham, MD 20706
www.rowman.com
www.downeastbooks.com

Distributed by NATIONAL BOOK NETWORK

Copyright © 2022 by Susan Hand Shetterly

Library of Congress Cataloging-in-Publication Data
Names: Shetterly, Susan Hand, author.
Title: Notes on the landscape of home / Susan Hand Shetterly.
Description: Lanham, MD : Down East Books, an imprint of Globe Pequot
Trade division of The Rowman & Littlefield Publishing Group, Inc.,
[2022] | Includes bibliographical references. | Summary: "In an age of
restlessness, Shetterly explores what it means to stay in one place by writing
about the things she finds in the natural world around her home on the
ragged edge of the continent"—Provided by publisher.
Identifiers: LCCN 2022007269 (print) | LCCN 2022007270 (ebook) |
ISBN 9781684750290 (cloth) | ISBN 9781684750306 (ebook)
Subjects: LCSH: Shetterly, Susan Hand | Natural history—Maine—Prospect
Harbor. | Nature conservation—Maine.
Classification: LCC QH31.S497 A3 2022 (print) | LCC QH31.S497 (ebook) |
DDC 508.741—dc23/eng/20220322
LC record available at https://lccn.loc.gov/2022007269
LC ebook record available at https://lccn.loc.gov/2022007270

ALSO BY SUSAN HAND SHETTERLY

Seaweed Chronicles
Settled in the Wild
The New Year's Owl

Books for Children

The Dwarf-Wizard of Uxmal
Raven's Light
Muwin and the Magic Hare
The Tinker of Salt Cove
Shelterwood
Swimming Home

FOR MY GRANDSONS
Giles,
Levin,
and
Marsden

and in memory of Wayne Newall

At the still point of the turning world . . .
there the dance is . . .

—T.S. ELIOT

CONTENTS

CONTENTS

PREFACE

THIS BOOK IS ABOUT living in one place, with its bay and woods and wildlife. A number of the chapters I wrote during the pandemic, and they reflect aspects of the time. Others are about the inheritance of a deep human culture we hold in Maine, and still others are about native wildlife, altered habitats, climate change, and the virtues of building a managed commons. Some lead away from this Down East coast, but they come back.

I have taken the epigraph for the book from Eliot's great poem, "Burnt Norton:"

> At the still point of the turning world . . .
> there the dance is . . .

This is a still point for me, a small neighborhood in a small town. The dance, I believe, is between the individual lives of the many species that live here, the community we make together, and time.

A BEGINNING

A BEGINNING

ONE

CHILDREN OF ORION

ON A CLEAR NIGHT the sky is black, and the constellations burn brightly here. No lights from a nearby town, no headlights from a stream of cars obscure Orion, the great hunter who pledged to rid the world of wild animals and was felled by the sting of a single scorpion. As I write this it's the heart of winter. Orion with his belted sword moves slowly to the west during the long hours of darkness. If the air is drifting onshore, up the ledges, across the fields, and into the woods, you can stand outside in the breathtaking cold and smell the salt from the bay.

My first home was my parents' apartment on Bleeker Street in New York City. Later, we moved to an old colonial in Connecticut with woods and fields and a little stream, and later still we spent a few enchanted years in Mallorca. But the truth is I grew up in a cabin on a 65-acre woodlot half a mile from a working harbor in Down East Maine, if growing up means learning something about how to live in the world. I moved there with my husband and first child. I was 29 years old. The life I had lived before, all that was tender, funny, painful and loving, frightening or deeply beautiful, was preface and preparation for the years I spent learning how to manage a life that was both practical and good for the spirit, and exploring what was left of the wild in this cutover land.

The natural world and my exposure to it grew into a solid thing. I was a part of something bigger than I was, that was subtle and complicated, and I paid attention. If you pay attention to the land where you live, as many of us already know, you enter into conversation with it, until it becomes a voice inside you and some of the boundaries between you and it dissolve. That woodlot and the village around it were teaching places for me, as home places all over the world have gifts to teach when we are alert to the pieces that fit together to make them whole, or when we note the pieces that are missing that indicate, in some ways, big or small, that they're broken.

My experience is not unusual. People bond to where they live. Over time, they witness change and notice what endures. More often now, I worry that these places may not last in a recogniz-able way beyond our own lives, which means that they will not be teaching others the things we know and the things we still hope to learn. On the other hand, the work to save land and water and air and the species that have evolved along with them—on a large scale, and in our own backyards—changes how people relate to what's left of the wild and what they teach their children. That's a start.

After ten years, my family and I moved from the village to a small town half an hour to the west, where I live today. The bay here is shallow, and the tide sweeps in over mud, and the stone at the shore is ancient schist, a metamorphic rock, older than the pink and gray granite, melted by heat and formed in a slow cooling, that faces the water at the village shore we left. They are both part of the story of this coast.

When I began to learn about the place where I'd arrived, a friend had left us his binoculars and my father gave me his old, scuffed Peterson's bird guide. If I was free, I'd grab the binoculars and the guide and go to the harbor shore, or walk along the skidder trails in the woods, or out to the ponds or the nearby marsh. Each was different. I didn't know a fir from a spruce, a black duck from a mallard, but I was patient. I kept at it, and I depended on what our neighbors told me about this land and water, and on books

I ordered from the local library, and what I saw and heard and smelled and touched on my own.

Our neighbors, whose families had lived here for a long, long time, told us that out on the village's Grand Marsh farmers had cut salt hay for winter feed for horses and cattle in August a hundred years before we arrived. When we hiked it, it wasn't farmers or the ghosts of farmers and their horses we saw, but short-eared owls. The birds would pop up out of the marsh grass and flap away, low over the worn dikes and slick channels.

One of my favorite Henry David Thoreau quotes is "I have travelled a good deal in Concord." Although he'd walked Cape Cod three times, canoed the Concord River, and come to Maine to climb Katahdin, canoe the East Branch of the Penobscot, and go up the Allagash, what he's getting at is that if you want to learn from the land you live on and the life it supports, including human life, you have to do what he taught himself to do at Walden, which was to settle in, go deep. Watch how your neighbors respond to and work with the land. Walk into its corners and its broad stretches at different times of day, in all seasons, and you will begin to read it with a proficiency that may surprise you.

There are people who have learned a lot about their home places in the world: when the ramps growing under the white pines down by the river are ready to pick, for instance, or when the black-capped chickadee first sings its spring song, and the relief a person can feel when that initial heavy snow of the year pulls a curtain down on all unfinished autumn chores. These are the people who also notice the first small changes of a warming world on their own patch of ground.

I think of my neighbors looking out their windows this time of night. And my mind wanders to places far away, and people I have never met, who love where they live: The Amazon River villages that aren't damaged yet, and the people in their homes by the river at night listening to the swish of the moving water, and the young kids looking up at the night sky. Or the tundra in Alaska, barren except for ptarmigan, Arctic foxes, and snowy owls, the owls drifting over the deep white landscape under brilliant pinpricks of shining stars, past the homes of people sleeping. Or sometimes I remember the little fishing village in Mallorca, where the fishermen took their boats out on the water into the night. Standing onshore, we watched the strings of small lights tied to the gunnels moving away from the harbor in their own tight constellations beneath the stars and listened to the soft purr of the motors.

I look up into the sky at night now and think of people all over the world in the comfort of their homes, and the land and water stretching out around them, dark and full of living things.

We're nourished by what's left of wildness, by the knowledge that we belong among other species—both animal and plant—and to lose them would be to lose something we honor in ourselves. When the stars wake me up on especially clear cold winter nights—it's their silence, I think, and their needle-sharp points of light that disturb my sleep—he's there, the hunter who thought we'd be better off all by ourselves on this Earth.

TWO

APPRENTICESHIP

WE MAY NOT RECALL the list of American presidents in the correct order, who followed whom, and we may have forgotten most of the lines to *Tintern Abbey*, no matter that we studied Wordsworth's poem feverishly a long time ago (but remember why it's important: it was here he wrote "Nature never did betray the heart that loved her . . .") We may have forgotten what Hamlet said when he found the gravediggers at work and was handed Yorick's skull, but despite the loss of some detail we once knew, when we pay attention and work at it, we learn how to learn things. That's what an education teaches.

When you're in your twenties, you're an apprentice. I arrived at the Maine coast then, a back-to-the-lander who'd never learned from land, but who was about to. I arrived with a husband and our one-year-old son. We had everything before us. I think of those years, and I remember others who came from away and settled in places nearby and began trying to build a life in a village that hadn't seen an influx of people like us, ever. Many failed. What surprises me is how many succeeded. When we did succeed it was because we paid attention and worked hard. And, frankly, because the people in the village who knew things we did not were gracious enough to teach us. First, there was the wood cutting and twitching and splitting and drying for the stove. Then there was the food: bread making, putting up vegetables for winter, visiting the boats at the dock for the catch of the day. And there was the winter. What can

I say about the winter? The first year, in February, I wore two wool hats to bed at night, and held our son against me to keep him warm under piles of blankets. When our daughter was born, I did the same.

My husband's dream was to be a painter. Mine was to be a writer. But to get to those dreams, we had to figure out how to take care of ourselves and our children, make some money, and not freeze to death or burn the cabin down.

For me, there was everything to learn—how to live, how to write, how to be in this woodland and begin to understand how it worked. We stumbled a lot and we got better. We got to know the people, the birds, the shore, how to grow food, how to—and this is important—talk with the people who lived here. Who, in fact, made this village what it was. What I mean is we needed to learn to listen more than talk. People in the village, back then, didn't go on and on. They said what they had to say with, often, a quick intake of breath and few words. Like hammering a shingle onto the side of a house. A couple of strikes, and that's it. It's done.

I can't forget that first year and my trips to the laundromat in the town next door. I've told this story before, but for me it is one of my teaching stories, and so I will tell it again: I'd arrive with pillowcases of diapers; muddy, stained work clothes; and once, in the fall, after we had been told to cover our tomato plants with blankets at night so that they wouldn't freeze, an armload of blankets I had gathered that morning from the garden when it got too chilly for tomatoes, even with the blankets. When I set them down in front of women twice my age sitting on metal chairs against the wall of the laundromat, waiting for their machines to be done, and whose husbands were the fishermen I'd met in the village, they stared at the floor. Following their gaze, I looked down. At least five garter snakes were slipping out from beneath the blanket folds, a bit stunned from the cold and the trip in the car.

"Poor things!" I cried, and began grabbing them up, shoving them into the carpetbag purse I'd bought at a yard sale. "Poor things!", I said again, as if the women hadn't heard me the first time. They sat, stone-faced.

"I'll be back," I shouted and left with my writhing purse, drove home, returned the snakes to the frost-damaged tomato patches, and then went calmly back to the laundromat. When I got there, the women were either folding their clothes, with their backs to me, or sitting where they had been sitting when I left, no expression at all on their faces. As if the snakes had never happened. I went about the washing.

I got to know them better, and then I knew they'd had a riotous laugh at my expense, as well as saying some abrupt, and perhaps even brutal, words about people from away who seemed not only clueless, but nuts.

When I came to Maine, the first room I wrote in was a tiny former chicken shed, set back in the second-growth hardwoods where we lived, a mile down Pond Road from the harbor. The shed was all mine. The chickens lived in the bigger shed a few yards away, closer to the cabin. I'd found an old Remington typewriter at a yard sale, managed to whack a few boards up to the shed's two-by-fours for a table, and borrowed a chair from the kitchen.

It was perfect.

This was a summer-only writing space, but those summers seemed almost endless, with enough time in them to teach myself to begin to find my voice as a writer and to test what I believed. What to write about wasn't, somehow, a question.

My husband and I had moved into the unfinished cabin on the woodlot, five minutes by bike from the working harbor. Eventually, we had two thriving children, twelve chickens, a cat, and two dogs. I was learning all that I could, as people do when everything is new, about where I was in this world, its trees and wild birds and animals, fish and fishermen, the women who knitted mittens for the village children for Christmas, and the big salt marsh where saltmeadow cordgrass grew.

I would write about where I lived as I discovered it.

A maple sapling threw a delicate branch across the window of the chicken shed. During the day, as the light changed with the sun's arc, the tree's green patterns changed and fluttered and shone. I had read, and taken to heart, Virginia Woolf's *A Room of One's Own*, and I knew that to be a writer, one needed a private space and some unencumbered time to spend in it. And one needed the belief that to write, even to write badly (because that is what one does a lot of as a beginning writer), was okay. My husband and I spelled each other, and our children played in the gardens and in and out the open doorways of the cabin, loose and free, and somehow, luckily, safe.

I had also read E.M. Forster's books, one of which is *A Room with a View*. It is about breaking convention in order to find out what one loves. All his books embrace the imperative of connecting to something outside oneself, and of taking a brave chance on the wide world. Only connect, he writes.

At night, by kerosene lamp, sitting at our kitchen table, I read Thoreau, Leopold, Abbey, Muir—learning the fundamentals of the environmental movement. Their words and the direction they gave are with me still. And I read E.B. White because he is the essayist, the best teacher of style, and he lived only a short distance down the coast in an old farmhouse with a big barn that, he reassured his readers, sheltered spiders in summer and fall.

The sound of the Remington, the roller bar when I spun it, the arm when I flung it decisively, and the gleeful act of pulling a finished sheet of my own prose out of the machine, gave me a sense of who I might be becoming. And I had met a man who held a license to rehabilitate wild birds. He taught me to take care of young birds—nestlings and fledglings.

Once I was given a naked hatchling in a nest as neat as an English teacup that had fallen out of an elm in Castine, an upscale old town with a prerevolutionary history about two hours southwest of where we lived. The bird survived, attended by me and my children, and became a red-eyed vireo. It lived in the shed, often perching on me as I wrote. As a fledgling, noisy and energetic, it needed more space, and I knew I had to release it soon. But when, exactly?

One late afternoon I turned from the Remington to find an adult red-eyed vireo perched on the maple branch, staring in at the window. My vireo stared back. Neither moved. Quietly, I approached the window and unlatched it. The young bird hopped onto the sash, then out onto the branch. The older bird reached forward through the leaves. Bill to bill, they touched. The young one pulsed its wings very slightly, and they flew off.

Only connect: This was how my life grew toward the lives around me.

THREE

LITTLE MOOSE ISLAND

FROM THE MAINLAND to Little Moose Island in Schoodic Harbor, a person has to know the time of low tide before crossing the land bridge. If you get it right, you step carefully over the cobbles slick with algae and trek up the basalt dikes to the island's granite ledge.

There were times I got the tide wrong by about half an hour and waded with my two kids through the chilly water submerging the cobbles on our way back. Sometimes it was above their knees, and I held their hands to keep them from slipping and falling in as they grasped mine and held on tight. When we reached the car, we turned the heat up full blast for the short ride home. The water this far Down East, that far out in the bay, was never warm. Those were the years we lived in Prospect Harbor, in the cabin in the woodlot, and I took my children out to the island, or came by myself following its trails through the heath to the point, a rubble of glacial rock and driftwood, to stand at the end of it, looking out over the water that went on, as far as I could see, forever.

As you move Down East, you come to shorelines of granite, extrusions in pink or gray folds, some as large and as gently inclined as the backs of whales, others broken into huge block-like chunks. Once, hiking with my son and daughter-in-law out on Wass Island, the granite, smooth and gray against the gray water, the sky, gray, with only a tinge of blue at the horizon, I was nearly knocked flat by its gorgeous monotone grandeur, its rejection of all adornment. But then I thought of my daughter-in-law, who comes from Virginia, where green overwhelms the land and seems to reach far into the sky, and where the tones of color and the textures of the landscape are filigreed and deep. It occurred to me she might find it rather empty here.

Little Moose is fifty-four acres, located, with Big Moose Island, alongside the Schoodic Peninsula. They are part of the Acadia National Park System, which owns these 2,366 acres of islands and shoreline. That should mean they have inviolate protections. They do. Except from the effects of a changing climate.

For me, Little Moose is both whetstone and touchstone. Over time, as I have returned to walk it and let in its familiar beauty, like a whetstone it hones away the inessentials I carry. They fall like shavings from the blade of a knife, giving me the sharp fact of myself in the world. And a touchstone because I trust it. Walking here reminds me to love the work I do, the life I've made.

I came back again during the drawn-out days in the late fall of the COVID year. A fog drifted above the water and the island shore. It tasted of salt and seaweed, and I remembered, as I always seem to do, that my kids and I picked rose hips from the rugosa bushes that grow on the cobbled banks when we lived here. We hung them to dry over the woodstove for winter tea. I reminded myself that one February afternoon, when my son was less than a year old, I carried him in a backpack in a snowfall sweeping across the island and caught sight of a running fox—an orange dash through a veil of snowflakes. There was something about the fox, the snow, and the warm child against my back that made that time, that life, beautiful. I also remembered leaving the cabin, selling it, and moving to the town farther south. That year I had started writing a book instead of articles for magazines and newspapers. I missed the familiar village, the cabin, the island, and it was the year my marriage began to fall apart. Returning to Little Moose, I hiked it with a mourning fervor, determined to find within the losses a life that would emerge that would be good.

This time I was looking for the sort of correction and reassurance the island had given me before, and what I got, instead, was a quiet, persistent sense of urgency. If a warming climate has created stresses on the island, I can't spot them yet. And that's the trouble: changes, in many places, are incremental. They arrive like a whisper, trailing catastrophe from failing systems somewhere else. And before you know it, the whisper has become a shout. But it seemed to me as I hiked the island that the spruces were thriving and the creeping juniper and the bayberry still scented the air when I brushed against them along the narrow trails. Little Moose also has a gathering of black crowberry and three-toothed cinquefoil. Under the full brunt of weather, they, too, find refuge. Reaching the far end, and looking out at water that goes straight on, uninterrupted, to somewhere between the border of France and Spain, I went over in my mind what I know has changed along this part of the coast.

I had stopped to watch a greater yellowlegs at East Pond, a circle of mud and rocks and rockweed alongside the island. The bird, a late migrant down from its muskeg nesting ground, was doing that wonderful yellowlegs tipping—forward and back—as if it were a pitcher of cream at a busy tea party. It darted here and there, stabbing its long bill into the water, snatching up small prey. Then it flew off, with a high three-note cry, and was gone.

This species of shorebird will lose both nesting and wintering territory. You can see maps of its nesting range tightening as the boreal forests slowly slip away here and the taiga slowly opens up to trees. And its winter habitats, along the sloughs and marshes of the lower Midwest and the South, are being eaten up by drought and development. What was once ample nesting and wintering grounds are turning into ribbons. But the greater yellowlegs may be one of the luckier shorebirds.

Looking out at the restless pitch of the water in front of me, I remembered the shorebirds that had already migrated through, the semipalmated sandpipers, the least sandpipers, the semipalmated plovers, and others that stop to feed on mudflats along this coast in the late summer and early fall. I've seen them many times, holding binoculars to my eyes and drawing their bodies up close as they lean forward and poke their bills into the gritty, seaweed-draped shallows on a falling tide. For thousands of years, these shorebirds have flown extraordinary distances from South America and other faraway places, up the Atlantic flyway to the high Arctic to nest where food has been abundant and predators few. Then before you know it, they fly back again, on their way down.

Famously, Delaware Bay makes a critical difference in the lives of some of them. They have keyed to it in the spring, to the feast of millions of eggs buried in the sand at the edge of the water by thousands upon thousands of spawning horseshoe crabs. It was this historic refueling stop, this cornucopia of eggs that pop out of the sand in a rough tide or when they're scratched up by yet more spawning crabs, that kept the birds' journey going, kept them, quite simply, alive.

But the Delaware horseshoe crab population is stunningly fragile and dropping. For decades, there was no regulation of the harvest taken for bait, for compost material, and for biomedical testing, and the take today is only partially restricted. Horseshoe crabs have been the gold standard against which our vaccines are screened for pathogens. Many of us probably wouldn't be here without them. Especially now, during COVID. When the crabs are caught as they come to shore to spawn in the spring, and sold to a lab, each is strapped to a harness, bled, and then returned to the sea, but too many die from the ordeal or are too weak to spawn. This practice of extracting lysate from their blood to test the purity of our vaccines was once an essential safety precaution for us, but it is no longer necessary, and hasn't been for years: a synthetic substitute works just as well, without using a single crab. However, laboratories are reluctant to switch, to give up the traditional methods, and the changeover has been, at best, too slow.

When the shorebirds along the East Coast flyway arrive on their Arctic nesting grounds, if they get beyond the bottleneck of Delaware Bay, they may find that native sedges such as cotton grass and hundreds of other short, tough plants in which they hide their nests have been flattened or uprooted by flocks of snow geese. In these degraded habitats their eggs and young are especially vulnerable to predators.

The numbers of the sleek, beautiful geese have grown by more than 300 percent since the mid-1970s, due, mainly, to waste corn in the industrial fields of the Midwest where they spend the winter feeding. As the geese population skyrockets, shorebird species decline.

Full protection for horseshoe crabs in Delaware Bay and keeping snow geese from waste corn in the Midwest aren't easy problems, and yet solving them would allow our shores and the tundra nesting grounds to keep doing just what they do best in the spring and fall, which is to give birds a place to feed and food to eat and safe places to nest. But the problem that confounds all others is the changing climate, the rising seas, the melting permafrost, the fragility of the tundra, the taiga, and the fierce storms in the spring and fall during migration.

I am teaching myself to walk this island as pilgrim and penitent. Pilgrim, to learn how to do things differently, penitent, for the times I have failed to understand. To the end of the island and back is only about a mile, but I imagine, as I hike from the mainland, that I am starting out on an adventure that is big, akin to walking El Camino de Compostela, as if I were crossing through northern Spain, leaning forward—a bit like a shorebird does when feeding—into the wind. It is a journey of discipline and gratitude. It allows me the space to come to terms with this: the little world of the island has been for many of us a constant, against which time, as we experience it, seems to have left only the most cursory of marks. But we've come, at last, to the end of the old dispensations.

It will take people from across the world together, with hard work and little time, to protect this place into the future. It will take my effort to learn how to support their wild places, most of which I will never see—jungle riverbank, mangrove swamp, sequoia old growth, a deep stretch of polar ice, the summer tundra.

A SHEAF
OF DAYS

~

FOUR

WONDERFUL THINGS

MY FIVE-YEAR-OLD GRANDSON caught an elver in the stream behind his house. He held it in the cup of his two hands, and his whole being was lit up with wonder and concern. Concern, because he hoped he hadn't hurt it. Which he hadn't. And wonder at this live being, its strange, jet-black beauty.

I like to think that we are all experiencing a moment like this. Perhaps a hummingbird will set it off, or the long trill of a winter wren, an alewife school moving steadily upstream, an osprey on its nest, or a newly arrived elver. I hope that these beings whose lives have touched ours during the time of COVID fear and isolation will inspire us now to change the way we share the Earth with them. We've been given a pause. We have had time to notice that wild lives love their lives as much as we love ours.

The American eel connects the Gulf of Maine directly to the Sargasso Sea that lies over a thousand miles south of here, east of Bermuda, a vast archipelago of floating seaweed islands in the Atlantic Ocean, a special place of such abundance, attracting so many species of wildlife that some scientists call it the ocean's rain forest. It's there that mature eels spawn and die, we assume, although no one has conclusively ever found either a dead or dying eel at the Sargasso. What have been found, however, are tiny leaf-shaped larvae that drift in the seaweed and then move away, northward, carried on the Gulf Stream. Some of them reach the Gulf of Maine, change into glass eels, and then into black elvers that ascend our rivers and streams. They, like alewives, link our coastal waters to our inland ponds and lakes, turning individual habitats into beads on a string.

The elvers grow into eels that can spend decades in fresh water. We call them yellow eels. But at some point—we don't know the trigger—they are ready to go. They turn silver-bellied and black-backed. Their eyes grow big. Together, and one by one, on chilly, wet, autumnal nights, these silver eels start their journey to the sea. And they're gone.

Not so long ago, people thought eels sprang from earthworms, or out of the hairs of horses' tails, or from chunks of mud that fell into the water. Today we know better, but these fish still keep their secrets, still make their long journeys, still need the Sargasso Sea, our bays and streams and ponds.

I write this because the Sargasso's seaweed is overharvested, polluted with plastics, and the warming of the water is affecting the trajectory of the Gulf Stream. If it wanders off, away from the coastline, it will take those tiny, leaf-shaped larvae with it. I write this because Maine is the only state along the Eastern Seaboard that harvests elvers as if there were no tomorrow.

Nations are just beginning to work together to try to figure out how to save the American and European eels in the hope that we all carry for a more generous future. Nations, of course, are made up of communities, and communities are made up of individuals who care.

Maybe your heart doesn't warm to the American eel. That's fine. Many species need our advocacy. What about the grasshopper sparrow? Or the monarch butterfly? What about the right whale or the little brown bat or the upland plover? In these days of stillness and grief, with the coming together of a crisis in climate and the COVID crisis, we've been given time apart to figure out what needs to heal and how we might go about it. We've been given time to think about that kid standing on the stream bank, not sure if what he holds in his hands is the most wonderful thing he's ever seen in his entire life, but thinks it may be.

FIVE

THE SURRY FOREST

IT STARTED WITH an offer to sell. An Italian family had bought a 2,200-acre tract of cutover woodland in my town of Surry, which sounds a bit odd to begin with, but it's true. They bought it for an investment, and in 2014, their American representative contacted Blue Hill Heritage Trust. The family's interests were turning elsewhere, and they had already harvested much of what was left of the timber.

I was on the board of the Trust then, as was Pam Johnson, my friend and a lover of wild plants and wild places.

Would we be interested?

Pam and I drove in over a hard-used and insubstantial gravel road disassembling in the July heat, leaking pebbles into old piles of slash. The forest looked like forests do when they are logged quickly and repeatedly, the firs and spruces pinched tightly together, some healthy white pines towering above them, skinny red maples and poplars and birches in want of a good thinning. We left the car and trekked in by foot, reaching one of the biggest beaver dams I have ever seen. It came up to my shoulders, topped with beveled sticks and well-chinked with mud and stones. Water poured over it in thin silver rivulets and swept into a little sun-washed meadow beyond.

The loggers had left this beautiful cup alone. Pam was beside herself. She waded into the waist-high meadow naming, in Latin, the plants she recognized.

"Why don't you tell me in English?" I asked.

"No!" she shot back. "Because Latin names them for everyone. English doesn't." And on she waded into the wet meadow. I remember thinking she's vanishing in front of me, turning into a reed or a royal fern, transforming herself and spouting Latin.

Before we could make an offer, an American logging company stepped in. The land went to them. Two years later, that company approached the Trust.

We drove out to visit the land again, this time on a March afternoon, and Pam was already ill. Being ill, for her, was beside the point. The point was the possibilities left in this huge, worked-over place.

If it was bad the first time, this time we trudged through a landscape with spotty bunches of tilting trees, hills of slash, and dirt gouged by enormous harvesters.

We came to where the beaver dam had stood. It was gone, of course, as was the meadow.

"I hate this," I said.

Pam was undeterred. She wanted a second chance. "Land comes back," she said. "It'll come back."

At the next lands meeting of the Trust, I spoke against buying the land. Pam lobbied hard to buy it, and at last we did. The next spring, I walked in by myself, stood in the thick, unfurling brush, and found—how could this be?—that it was filling up with birdsong.

Sandy Walczyk and I hiked in past the rock bearing the brass plaque in memory of Pam, who insisted there was life still to be found here. It was July and Sandy is the Trust's new forest manager. She's young. She's got a keen eye and a big heart for this resurgent place, and she tells me that managing it is her dream job.

"How's that?" I asked.

"It's been cut hard, obviously, and trees grow slowly, so you need patience, but this forest is resilient. When you manage a forest like this, it starts to feel as if you know it and it knows you. I love getting my hands in it. I love hiking through it. There are some gorgeous wetlands deep in here, with beautiful maples and big pines."

She tells me that she wants it to be a teaching place for this community to learn good stewardship. In spring she and a group of volunteers carried in shovels and planted over two thousand trees, young saplings. And, she says, they've set up a camera to catch the animals passing through. They've seen black bears, moose, coyotes, and bobcats. The land is alive with them, she tells me.

She wants to show me some of the saplings they've planted, so I follow her into brush and pin cherries. We peer through the green mix for the newly planted hardwood trees. And we find them, their distinctive leaves on such tender, beginning stalks: *Quercus rubra, Acer saccharum, Betula alleghaniensis.*

SIX

NORTH BEND ROAD

I MISS COUNTING ALEWIVES. The summer has bloomed into a tangle of busyness, and I look back now to the simplicity of early spring, the days cold and wet, the trees just leafing out, the warblers just back, and the water of Patten Stream pouring under the bridge at North Bend Road, gurgling and swishing along the banks like a swimming animal seeking its way to the bay.

For twelve years a group of us, citizens of this town, have worked to restore a safe passage for alewives, a species of herring, so that when they come back from deep water to our early spring bay, they can move up Patten Stream to their natal pond to spawn. A weir and pool construction, a series of rising steps created out of granite blocks with iron rods to stabilize them against the damage of pummeling water at ice-out, has lifted the water level step by step to meet the culvert under Route 172, just above the bay. The fish swim easily though the culvert now, which they hadn't been able to do for years.

After that they must fight their way up a natural falls, around or through a number of beaver dams, and glide beneath North Bend Bridge to the outlet to Patten Pond, past the place where I or someone else sits on rocks in the shadow of the bridge and counts them. When the run is over, we send the numbers to the Maine Department of Marine Resources.

From one bank to the other, we have laid a row of white bags filled with sand in the streambed. The fish swim over the bags and that makes them easy to see. I count by tens. Ten. Twenty. Thirty.

Each phalanx of fish, one after another, whether twenty or a hundred fish or more, is all business. Their blunt noses point upstream, their sleek gray backs pack together, their tails move in unison, side to side. This is our town's magnificent migration.

To witness this part of the life cycle of these essential wild fish that almost disappeared from our lives, to have helped them to flourish, brings some of us near tears. I have seen photographs of caribou galloping across the tundra, the dust rising from their hooves. Here there is no sound. No dust. This migration is the silent and sleek imperative of homing fish.

Neighbors who keep this early spring vigil love it as much as I do for the gentle pause in their day, for warbler song around us, and the sound of the water, and the occasional car over the bridge that makes the girders hum, and for the proof, right here in our own town, that if we give what's wild half a chance, it will, as these fish teach us each spring, do the hard part.

This year the fish came late. The water out of the pond was too cold, and there were days when no one saw a single fish. We spent our individual time watching the light tannin water streak by and letting ourselves ease into springtime under the bridge: the clouds, the rain, the sun, the wind, the phoebes building a nest on one of the girders.

Philip Booth, the noted Castine poet, wrote a poem titled "How to See Deer" that gives me a dictum I carry: "Expect nothing always." That's the way to see. If you allow for any possibility, if you demand no certain outcome, then you take in everything that's around you. Sometimes it's fish. Sometimes it's a female yellowthroat picking up a bit of sedge for her nest. Sometimes it's just the water flowing by. And that's fine.

SEVEN

ODE TO AN APPLE TREE

I FIND MYSELF GOING out in the early morning to stand next to my apple tree to see if a few of the buds have swelled. Sometimes I test them with my fingers. What I am testing for is a little life, a bit of juice.

This beloved tree keeled over in a northeast storm last fall. Its once ample crown is crammed against the bole of a spruce. Two brown apples still dangle from the highest branches that the deer couldn't reach, and that the birds, for some reason, have rejected.

Most of the roots are thrust into the air like the fingers of a monstrous arthritic hand. I am not sure what I would do if some of the buds were in contact with a root still anchored in the ground, and the hydraulics of springtime and sap flow kicked in. Can you put a tree like this back together?

What kind of apple tree is it? I don't know. We planted it years ago when it was a skinny stick with a thatch of young roots that we bought in a bundle of dormant plants from the Soil and Water Conservation sale in Ellsworth. Once in the ground it took off, withstood deer and porcupines, outlived a flurry of sapsuckers and tent caterpillars. It grew into a big tree, a centerpiece in the yard that held one's gaze all year long.

In winter I hung birdfeeders from its lower branches; it gave the small birds cover from hawks. In spring, it flowered like a bride. Flocks of cedar waxwings came to eat the petals. In summer it was a hangout for warblers, chickadees, blue jays, robins, doves, and nuthatches busy hunting insects in the leaves or resting within the branches. The green apples, no bigger than chickpeas at the start, grew and turned a streaky deep red. By fall, my neighbors came to pick, as did I. We got buckets, and there were so many left. The apples were tart, sweet, and they made the best applesauce. The blue jays and the chickadees pecked at the leftovers. So did the robins. The red squirrels bit through the stems and carried apples away. Once a young porcupine tried to gnaw through the metal flashing I had wrapped around the trunk to protect the tree—from porcupines. It made a racket, and I chased it away in the dark with a hearth broom.

In early autumn mornings, with mist rising off the field, deer ate the new windfalls. I watched them chew, drooling apple juice, and saw the mouthfuls of apple move down their long gullets, as if they were giraffes.

My son gave me a pruning ladder to reach up into the heavy branches and cut away some of the weight they carried. But the tree seemed perfectly happy to me. I never used the ladder. Each year the tree reached upward and outward with a vigor I found exhilarating. A few lower dead branches were good for bird feeders and the splay of new branches in time grew heavy with fruit.

Above the wind, on the night of the storm, a sound filled this clearing like a gigantic sigh—a huge exhale of breath. At dawn I went out to pick a few apples for applesauce for breakfast and found my tree slumped on the ground like a beached whale.

It was a glorious tree. It was a magic tree that could feed everyone. But I was too proud of it to give it a sensible, cautious pruning. And pride goeth before a fall.

EIGHT

SPRING RAIN

LAST YEAR IN APRIL, with a flashlight in hand, I stood on the road by my house in an April rain in the dark. It was the sort of early spring nighttime rain that feels colder than snow, and I could see by the beam of the flashlight old snow crusts humped up in patches in the woods.

It was my job to look for frogs and salamanders that might have crawled out of their overwintering places and, slick with rain, they'd start crossing the road, lumbering toward their breeding pools. They're barely awake when they emerge. They're slow and, in the hand, they feel like living icicles. If I found some, I was to rally my neighbors and together we would usher them across, stopping cars, and lifting them toward where they were headed.

We have been learning about the dangers amphibians face: the diseases that sicken them, the destruction of habitat, the roads. And we wanted to do something to help.

By ten o'clock I hadn't found a single one—wrong night for this show—and I gave up and walked home. On my land, a shaggy woodlot of conifers, I have two ponds. They are small, shallow, and bursting with cattails and pickerelweeds and water lilies and blue flag that I have brought from other, bigger ponds and dug in, and although my ponds are tiny, the plants have taken root and thrive. I fancied myself a sculptor of sorts, carving out of mud and water lovely places I would make for the amphibians. The salamanders are, of course, silent, and the joy we find in them is to beam a flashlight into a pond bottom when they are doing their slow, circling mating dance. The joy of wood frogs and spring peepers is in their voices.

Spring begins in this woodlot with a male robin's sudden burst of territorial song and the male wood frogs' dry staccato counterpoint, somewhat like a bunch of black ducks quacking. And then the chorus of spring peepers begins, high-pitched bells ringing through the night.

A few days ago, I got in touch with a wetland biologist because over the years I have noticed that my ponds have slowly changed. It seems to me that fewer eggs are spawned, fewer polliwogs hatch from the egg masses, and of those that do, not many metamorphose into frogs. This worries me, and she has agreed to give me some practical pond advice. I no longer care that the pickerelweed and the blue flag and the water lilies are beautiful. I don't care that the cattails in a summer storm beat like the wings of a fast flock of birds. I care that the egg masses hatch, that the polliwogs have enough to eat, and that the froglets who step from the water onto land come back next spring to sing.

She's suggested that one of my ponds, shaded by softwoods to the south, may be too cold when the eggs are first laid, and that the upper pond, which dries out by June, before the larvae become frogs and salamanders and can safely leave it, needs fewer cattails, and perhaps a small dam to hold the water in.

That night of the hard spring rain a year ago, in the next town over, they had what is called a Big Night, lifting frogs and salamanders, hurrying them across a patch of road, sometimes even gathering throngs of amphibians into buckets and ferrying them to safety. Our Big Night here came about a week later, and we missed it.

But this year, on this road, we will try to get the timing right, and I will work on my ponds. Whatever we choose to love that's wild, it's likely these days that it needs some kind of help. And in small towns in this state, people who love frog song and salamander dance grab their flashlights and reflective vests and head out together to their neighborhood roads on the first hard rains to save, if they can, the singers and the dancers. To keep the dancing and the music going.

NINE

A WALK ON THE HEATH

A WALK ON A HEATH is not like a walk through the woods or along a stream or the bay. A bare expanse, a heath has caught all the wind, sun, sheets of rain, and layers of snow the sky has to offer. It's beautiful, if you accept the stillness it holds, its subtle gradients of green and gray and brown, and the sudden bursts of color you sometimes have to search for.

In March, three neighborhood friends and I hiked into Emerton Heath, a one hundred-acre expanse of low, tough shrubs in our town. The snow was mostly gone, but it was a lumpy place, with sheep laurel and leatherleaf sticking out of sphagnum hummocks frozen as hard as rocks, and bushes of rhodora and Labrador tea, their buds ready to flower in a spring warmth that hadn't yet arrived. There's something menacing but also exhilarating about hiking out onto a heath like this. You couldn't manage a run through it if you had to, and it's easy to lose your way, following the threads of deer trails, looking back at where you think you might have come from, which now seems far away and unfamiliar. Ahead you brace for something to show itself at the horizon: maybe the silhouette of a bull moose or a black bear, or, if it's foggy, you might let yourself imagine one of those haunted human spirits, their bodies preserved in layers of old wet sphagnum—the color of strong tea and terribly shrunken—the sort that might rise out of the depth of an Irish bog.

Down East, close to the ocean, is where you find many of the heaths of Maine. The Great Wass Island slope and raised bog, for instance, is one where a friend of ours, as a child, picked baked apple berries for his mother to put up for winter treats, and the Great Heath, near Columbia Falls, through which the Pleasant River runs, is another. To canoe it on a dry year is to move upstream within a scoured riverbed dug into the heathland by water, where you look directly up to see the sky, and the banks of the river are only a few yards from your face. Upon those banks grow turtlehead flowers and cardinal flowers in summer, and if the water is especially low, you paddle nearly six feet beneath the top of the land. It can make you feel a bit like a swimming turtle or a fish.

I love the sounds of the words that define heaths: bog and muskeg, from the Gaelic and the Cree, respectively, are words for heathlands that are mostly sphagnum; a lagg, from a Scandinavian root, is the wet moat encircling a heath; fen, from Old English, is a heath that receives some mineral groundwater, which makes it an easier place for some wetland plants to grow; peat, again from Gaelic, means decomposing muck. And the word *heath* itself, when I learned it in Prospect Harbor, where I used to live, was pronounced "hayth."

Years ago, Sally Rooney, an accomplished Maine botanist, brought a group of us to this heath, here in Surry, and stood among the assemblage of plants and stunted trees and explained to us how they worked together, nutrient-poor and living mostly on rainwater. Nonetheless, some of them were blooming at her knees with startling profusion, and she reached down to show us how to identify them by leaf and stem and flower.

My friends and I plan in late spring to haul picnic chairs and thermoses of tea, binoculars, and some hand lenses out over the lagg and settle down in the first few yards of the gentle rise where we can look straight across, almost to the horizon. We'll search for the palm warblers that like to nest in heaths, and the flycatchers, hawking for insects from the limbs of the short black spruces. But mostly we'll sit in the big silence of this big place, sip tea, and let the day move on to evening.

TEN

LEAVING THE LAND

BILL THAYER DIED last April, at age 82, while working in his woodlot with his horses and a logging arch.

When they arrived to live here in the '70s, he and his wife, Cynthia, named their place Darthia Farm. In time their Gouldsboro neighbors had taken to calling him "Farmer Bill." He was a man who loved his wife, his organic farm, his horses, and the deep and settled life he had built in this coastal town.

Thirty years ago, he and Cynthia sat down at their kitchen table with representatives from Frenchman Bay Conservancy and wrote up a conservation easement for the farm, guaranteeing, as much as anyone can guarantee anything, that it would be farmed into the future, passing from one farmer to another, cared for by each in turn. The barn, the two houses, the many outbuildings, the farm store, and the broad pastures, hayfields, and frontage on West Bay are now protected from all development.

Two decades later, Bill and Cynthia again sat down to plan for the future, this time with Maine Farmland Trust, and they finalized an agreement that would confer ownership of the farm to some young farmers looking for a place to start their own dreams. Shepsi Eaton and Elizabeth Moran became those farmers, arriving from Long Island with their two small children to learn from Cynthia and Bill the innumerable bits and pieces of how this place, with its cows, chickens, turkeys, sheep and pigs, CSA gardens, and woodlot works. Each farm is a particular, complicated arrangement.

Darthia Farm's demands woke Bill every morning at four to begin his day with feeding chores, then, according to season, the plowing, the haying, the training of horses, the fixing of machinery, the patching of stalls and pens and pasture fences, the cutting and hauling of winter wood, the butchering, or the milling of new boards for outbuildings.

He also became a town selectman, voted in term after term. Cynthia, a novelist, spun, dyed, and knitted wool from the sheep, put up jams and jellies; baked Christmas cakes from an old family recipe; and oversaw the gardens, their harvests, and sales. She made time to found Schoodic Arts for All, which brings performances and other activities to the area, and, along with Bill, threw hayride parties for the local elementary school children every winter.

Perhaps one of the most nurturing things they did was hire apprentices and teach them farming in exchange for labor. Many young people who had worked on the farm have settled nearby, helping to build a community that has enriched the landscape as well as the character of this peninsula.

I have known Cynthia and Bill from the days they first arrived, when they were brand new, learning to farm from others. How could they begin to know how much they would come to mean to those around them?

The day after Bill died, a former apprentice brought over the coffin he had built that morning out of pine planks. Women bathed and dressed Bill's body. A small group of family and neighbors set him into the coffin, lifted and carried it, and laid it in the wagon outside.

Shepsi hitched up Andy and Star, the two beloved Haflinger horses that, until then, had been tended only by Bill. There was something ceremonial about the way Shepsi handled them: a gentle, reassuring touch, the beginning of a new partnership. The horses began the procession with him at the reins. Family and friends walked behind the wagon up a gradual rise to the place where the grave had been dug, and Bill, now leaving the land to the next farmer, settled into it forever.

ELEVEN

THE PRESERVE

WE SAVED THIS TWENTY-TWO acres with its half-mile rocky ledge at the head of Morgan Bay, a sheen of mud before it at dead low, and at its back, the deep upland of softwoods and hardwoods that had not been cut in more than fifty years.

But we lost something, too. It was a secret place for us, neighbors who knew it in detail and in season. That it didn't belong to us was a fact we hardly considered because whoever owned it had forgotten it entirely and forever. Had forfeited it to us. Long enough to raise our kids close to it. Long enough for one of us to die, ashes tossed from this shore, carried by this tide.

In summer, sometimes we stepped away from our work to walk here alone, to stretch out on the dark schist ledge that held the day's accumulated heat, to listen to the chuck of the waves. Usually no one else was here. It was just one human, the warm and comforting rocks, the water moving in a rhythm like our own heartbeat, and the trees, because even on a still day, the murmur of the trees would be there.

On hot afternoons, if you had the time, you might walk the length of shore, strip, and dive naked into the blue-green full tide at Spruce Cove, a tiny, deep cup of water ringed by trees. In winter we took our children to the bay and sat bundled up in the dark, in the snow, flashlights off, the stars shining down as we named the constellations.

We were a small community, a handful of neighbors in owner-built houses, living close to abandoned farm fields and mixed woods and bay water. We grew into landscape, and it marked us. A community that began as back-to-the-landers in the '70s, hard-working, gray-haired now, we thought we owned some land we loved because we loved it for so long.

We didn't worry that it could be broken into lots, and second homes built on it for people who haven't stoked a fire in a wood-stove through a January night. Didn't worry, that is, until the inher-itors of the land, who were spread out across the country, came together on one essential point: it was time to develop and sell.

~~~~~~~

I step out my front door into the silence of early morning, twenty degrees, and take my snowshoes from the porch and head to the bay. A ring-billed gull flies at the lip of the midtide water. It slants away over the gray chop as I step onto the path at the shore. Seven long-tailed ducks swim alongside a raft of floating ice that extends from the eastern shore. The ice looks thin, mushy at the edges, and the ducks are following its margin, tail to beak. They are usually talkative, but this morning they have nothing to say. Somewhere in the woods to the south a chain saw starts, stalls, then starts again. The noise is far away, a soft purr. Behind me in the trees, a barred owl calls once.

Nights are not cold enough to freeze the water at the shore. Not yet. In this first week of the new year, sea smoke rises three miles down where the bay flares into the broader, deeper bay of Blue Hill. Out there, water is tendering its last summer warmth, and the Arctic air sucks it away in damp puffs and streaks, confusing the outlines of both shores.

I strap on the snowshoes, clamber across the slick milk-colored ice coating the ledge, and take the preserve path into the woods. No other human tracks preceded me. The soft new snow has fallen through the big trees in wads. It lies about eight inches deep over the old crust.

Blue squares nailed to the trunks of the trees mark the path's direction, but if I didn't have the bright squares to follow, I could follow in the tracks of two coyotes. The path has become a winter game trail used by the coyotes and deer and hares and foxes. This human intrusion, no more than two feet wide, prompts how animals choose to move through these woods—a thin, consequential scar.

Today little craters of snow, no more than ten inches apart at the left of the path, show me that a short-tailed weasel popped its head up, took a look around, then scooted under again making a tunnel through the cold, bright fluff.

This is the season when the preserve is almost always empty of people. But at ice-out, they return. In early summer, my neighbors and I bring down chain saws, hacksaws, clippers, and limbers to clear away the trees that have fallen across the path and to trim some of the young growth.

⌁

But back to the family that owned the land before it became a preserve. They had no road access. Discreetly, they phoned abutting neighbors proposing an outsized amount of cash if one or the other would provide a right-of-way for a development road. In the first go-round, everyone said no, but it wasn't over, because the owners phoned again with a promise of more money. They knew, and now we did too, that two-acre lots on twenty-two acres at the head of the bay would give them a gold mine.

After the second call, our neighbor, Hugh, called the other abutters and asked them to hold off on an agreement. He told them he wanted to see if he could raise money to buy the land as a preserve, a landlocked parcel, but there wasn't a chance if a right-of-way were given.

He went door to door to the people with substantial homes along the bay: "Do you want to lose the view of the head of the tide, the one that's still wild land?" They did not. It is quite a view.

In the evenings, after work, we gathered at kitchen tables and wrote letters to town officials and to more neighbors. We listed the reasons why a preserve on salt water, open to all, might contribute something of value to the town. We listed the mammals, birds, and the plants we had seen on the land and from the shore.

People sent us checks. They wrote notes telling us how much they valued our work. Then, one night, the owners informed Hugh that the family had decided to sell for $50,000.

"Are you sure?" I asked when he called with the news.

"I'm sure," he said.

"Maybe they said $500,000?"

"Well, it seems too good to be true, but they said $50,000—and we're close to raising that already."

At the final signing, the race to save this place looked almost easy. Our long-shot dream came true. The board of directors of the land trust in the next town, Blue Hill Heritage Trust, agreed to accept the title. One of the abutters gave an easement across his field for a narrow footpath that people could use.

Soon after the signing, I co-led a bird walk at the shore. We started off—an intrepid bunch—and it wasn't until later that I got a chance to speak to the reticent man who followed at the edge of the group.

"This was my family's land," he told me. "I'm here to see what you've done with it."

"And what do you think?"

"Well, you're doing a nice job, I suppose." He said. "But some of us felt cheated, you know. Some of us took it pretty hard."

What could I say to him? I said it was a precious gift we would always honor and protect. But I understood this gain was his loss, and for that I was sorry. How do you work to save wild land without hurting someone who may want to do something else with it? You don't.

We named it The Carter Nature Preserve, in honor of his family, although for those who felt cheated, it was probably just a painful reminder. We, the neighbors, became the preserve's caretakers. We cut the path to Spruce Cove. We marked it with the blue metal flags.

People came. They loved it. They brought picnics, dogs, cooking gear—one year, a tent, a clothesline, a plan to spend high summer here—and a yen for piling stones into little cairns and arranging large sculptures out of high-tide driftwood. Some brought dogs without leashes. Some brought packs of dogs. With sudden access to the woods by way of the path, the dogs took off. Their owners chased them, thrashing through the underbrush, or they just let them go.

We picked up garbage. We broke up rings of stones and charred wood. We disinvited campers.

When we sat down to work on a preserve policy that we found we needed here, we discovered we did not agree on what "preserve" meant. These were long meetings. Bringing to the table amorphous, often contradictory ideas, we argued them into a bare-bones list of rules we could agree on.

Norman, a neighbor who is a fine carpenter, made a glass box on a post with the list writ large: Leave the Preserve the Way you Found It: No fires; no camping; no overnights; carry out what you bring in; no dogs in the woods or on the woods path. (We honored the summer tradition of owners bringing their dogs to the rocks for a swim.)

But most people don't read signs. Or not this sign. We reworded it. We wrote "Please." We wrote "Thank you." We offered a hand-painted map of the preserve and the trail. We quoted Aldo Leopold.

One day in fall, I walked the footpath across the field as a tall, thin girl strode toward me carrying two black plastic garbage bags. We smiled as we passed each other. I glanced down. Her bags were crammed with beach heather, the entire plants, flowers, stems, leaves, and roots. This was no bouquet.

"You are not allowed to pick anything here," I told her.

"Yes, I can," she said. "These grow at the low-tide level so it's okay."

"What? Did you read the sign?"

"It's okay," she insisted.

"Picking anything on this preserve is not allowed," I pitched my voice low. "And, by the way, beach heather grows in and above high tide, as I am sure you know by this time." My voice was beginning to rise.

"Oh, shut up," she said, and walked away, swinging her bags.

When I knocked on his door, Norman opened it, took one look at me, and handed me a piece of paper towel to wipe my tears and a cup of tea to calm me down. We sat at his table. He couldn't help it: he was laughing—softly, sort of under his breath. And I began to laugh, too.

"Shut up," he said. "That's pretty good. You know, people haven't been taught to take care of land. They have no idea," he said. "They've been taught to take as much as they can and trash the rest. We've got to figure out how to get them to behave better."

"They never will," I said.

"I think they will," he said.

He was right. It didn't happen overnight. It took seasons, which turned into years. It took botany walks, bird walks, geology walks. It took working with school groups. A change of heart. All around us, the bigger picture was exposing the extent of damage to natural places all over the world. We read about small river tribes, woodland tribes, fishing villages, rural towns, all of them trying to protect their best wild places and failing.

Aldo Leopold's words printed on our sign are from 1949: "When we see land as a community to which we belong, we may begin to use it with love and respect." Years have passed. We still need to teach and learn this simple lesson.

There are no more heather rampages. No more dog packs. People I never met before pass by me when I walk the preserve and say, "Isn't this a wonderful place?"

On a late August afternoon, I was walking the rocks back to the road with my dog after a swim when I met a boy and his parents coming down the stone stairway we had built. They were local people from the next town. The mother carried her baby. The boy stopped to pat my deaf springer and then headed for the tide pool as his father looked across the water at the terns diving midtide.

The mother shifted her sleeping child and told me that her son had been in the school nature classes here, and he loved this place, and had tried all summer to get them to come.

"We don't get much time as a family," she said.

The father turned to me. "Are those Arctic terns or common?"

"I can't tell from here," I said. We both watched the half dozen birds diving as the boy showed his mother the slipper shells in the tide pool. Neither the father nor I had brought binoculars, but the man had good eyes.

"Common," he said after a bit. "I see the black tips on the bills." They were plunging and rising and shaking off and flying away with thin silver fish.

"It's nice here," he said, his gaze slowly following the shoreline. "As she said, we don't get much chance to get away, but my boy had a good time. He kept talking about it, so we thought we'd check it out."

I touched my springer lightly on the head between his ears, which means it's time to go, and nodded to the man.

"It's all yours," I said.

THE STRANGEST
FISHPOND

TWELVE

IN DREAMS BEGINS
RESPONSIBILITY

DURING THE PANDEMIC I had a recurring dream. It was set underwater, a vision blurred by shifting currents and the light, and I was in it, moving ahead with slow swimming motions. Kelps swayed like trees in a wind around me, and fish, weaving in and out of the seaweeds, went about their business as if I were not there, not watching them. Beneath me sea anemones waved stinging tentacles. And across an uneven ledge, mussels were packed together, their shells slightly open, their orange mantles endlessly rippling and ruffling as they syphoned water in and out. They looked like living rugs.

Into this dreamscape, a right whale lumbered through the seaweeds. A school of bluefin tuna tore into a school of herring, and shreds of herring floated slowly down. Big cod weaved their way through the kelps, beautiful, heavy-jawed fish, with fleshy barbells dangling from their chins, and clean, white lateral lines running the length of their bodies.

This dream is Cashes Ledge. It's a real place, about a hundred miles out into the Gulf of Maine, southeast of Portland. Sylvia Earle, the renowned oceanographer, has called it a "Hope Spot." What she means is that by fully protecting it, we can start to return the Gulf to some of its former health.

It has been stirred into life for me by underwater photographers whose work I have pored over. I've written about Cashes Ledge before, but it wasn't until this past COVID year, in my house back in the woods and close to the bay, in a period of quiet and contemplation as well as heart-stopping dread, that I spent time looking at photographs of Cashes on the Internet, getting to know it visually. This, I told myself, is real. This, I'd remind myself, is good.

Divers have taken these photographs to show people on land what a last best place can look like. They, and many others, are obviously passionate about the fecundity of the place—busy, colorful, with sudden bolts of life, and a slow, rhythmic background beat. On the edge of sleep, the scenes come back to me as my own dive. No photographer in sight. But, in the light of day, I will never tug on a wet suit, or strap on an oxygen tank and goggles and jump off a boat, floating down to touch the solid ground of the ledge as I so effortlessly do in the dream.

Awake, I remember that John Smith, in 1616, called the Gulf of Maine "the strangest fishpond I ever saw." It was a compliment. This Gulf, at thirty-six thousand square miles, somewhat enclosed by the way the land gently bows to the east and also by the high underwater moraines from the last glacier to the south, is like a huge pond. The cold currents within it have given it life. Although this Gulf is among the fastest warming bodies of salt water in the world, and that warmth circulates, causing changes in its currents, Cashes Ledge is still that spot of hope. In a year of so much death, knowing about its abundance kept me sane, kept dreams from turning into nightmares.

It's an ancient chunk of exposed mountain range with intermittent mud trenches. Five hundred and fifty square miles of it make up a zone that is semiprotected. Ammen Rock, the highest peak, a slab that catches the sunlight at forty feet below the surface, is bathed in a mix of currents where wild lives and forests of seaweeds swirl around it in such profusion, it rivals a thriving coral reef.

This was what the Gulf of Maine looked like in the first years of White Contact. Into the 17th and the 18th century, underwater areas of such richness were still commonplace. But Cashes is no nostalgic postcard of what used to be. It's a template for the future. Conservation biologists who know the Ledge will tell you it has become a nursery where native species grow up, spawn, and eventually spread out into the larger waters of the Gulf, repopulating them. It offers a model, a way to think about how to heal underwater places elsewhere that have been damaged, and scientists come to study it and to learn what it teaches in the job of repair. It is not off limits to all fishing, and constant pressure is put on regulators to reopen it for more kinds of gear, such as bottom trawls, and more boats.

During the pandemic, many of us welcomed a wider view of the natural world. It was the human silence that led us there. It was the precariousness we felt in our own mortal skin and the increasing assaults of a changing climate. The two weren't that far apart.

Why hasn't the Ledge been assigned an inviolate status in perpetuity, such as making it the second Marine National Monument in the North Atlantic? What can we do to support this effort others are working for? Dreams, made of flights of imaginative fancy, sometimes help us find our way. Divers and photographers, who are dreamers themselves, have shared with us what Cashes teaches, in our own homes, in front of our own computers, which is how beautiful the functioning wild can be.

W.B. Yeats, at the end of his life, wrote a poem which he titled *In Dreams Begins Responsibility*. It is an opaque poem, but it reflects the concerns he had written about before: Have I done the right thing here? Have I put my time on earth to fair and honest use? He doesn't answer the questions. He asks them.

THIRTEEN

THE BEAUTIFUL BONES

WE HUMANS SEEM PROGRAMMED to respond to the mix of function and beauty in successful evolutionary adaptations as we might to the curves of a Michelangelo sculpture or the chiaroscuro brushwork of Rembrandt's canvases. When I think of the cave paintings in Spain and France, I believe that a similar impulse—a love of function and beauty—drove these long-ago people living up against the wild to make their art by the light of a burning torch. Among the works they left are the running horse, the stalking wolves, the delicate strength of a deer's legs, the long-legged heron in flight, and those bison herds, boulders of muscle and postures of intractable stubbornness; and then, too, they outlined the human hand, shapely and proficient.

I stood in front of the skeleton of a bluefin tuna in a glass case on a wall in the lobby of the science building at the University of Maine at Machias, as my mind hurried over these things, this desire we have to celebrate the bodies around us that are honed by time to the tasks before them: to find food, to escape death, to mate. That bluefin, the bare architectural structure of a superb animal, touched me.

It was animals that gave us our first lessons in aesthetics, and that's why we scrawled their images onto stone. Many of them were good to eat, and we hunted them in small, armed packs, but we also loved to watch the way they moved through their lives.

Gayle Kraus has taught biology at the university for over forty years, but to watch her, you'd think she'd just arrived with the sort of energy and enthusiasm you'd expect of a professor at the outset of a promising career. She came, in fact, in 1980, with her mother, and bought an old farmhouse in town, where her mother lived to be 104, and Gayle earned a license to rehabilitate injured and abandoned wild birds and mammals.

I can imagine arriving as a freshman and starting out at this nook of a campus in the shire town of Washington County. What might you expect? If you took a class of Gayle's, you'd be caught up in her energy.

"I'm still learning. I'm still enthusiastic," she told me. "In part it's because of the fieldwork. We use a lot of animals in my classes that wash ashore, so I am always in a learning mode. It's not old for me yet. I don't know if it will ever be."

In 2007, a marine warden who knew she was looking for the bones of animals for her classroom work, called to tell her that a huge bluefin had come ashore in a marsh about an hour away. It was stranded, alive at first, but by the time she got to it, it had died and been scavenged. What was left had turned mushy in the August heat.

"It was maggot soup," she said. "I put on my gloves and went through all of it to get out every bone I could. Nothing was articulated—everything was falling apart."

The fish was about eight feet long. It had been chasing a school of smaller fish, most likely mackerel, through the inshore water on a high spring tide. She took what she could find back to the university, cleaned it up, and in 2011, she brought out the bones from where she had stored them, and proposed putting the skeleton together in a course she named Skeletal Articulation, an advanced semester for marine biology and environmental studies majors. Seven students signed up.

"We worked three to five hours every Friday. I told them, it will be awful, but let's try it! So, we did. And we problem-solved. We kept looking up information on bluefins. There wasn't much out there then. We'd find a lot on tuna steaks and sushi."

They worked closely together, fitting bone to bone as the semester wore on. "We used hot glue because we were just learning, and if we put some bones together incorrectly, we could simply use a hair dryer, melt the glue, take the bones apart, and try again. We couldn't put all the gill filaments back together—they were just too small—but we got about a hundred of them to fit. And the caudle tail of the fish—it's shaped like a new moon—we had to learn which bones went on which end. We were taking apart other fish, like bass, to get some clue. But it didn't help. They're not alike. In the end, we learned so much. Now I can look at a tuna fin ray and guess pretty accurately where it might go." By the last day of the semester, they had assembled the bones, and it was done.

"Terribly frustrating and terribly exciting," Gayle said.

An Atlantic bluefin tuna larva, freshly spawned and floating in the Gulf of Mexico, is tiny. You could hold a couple dozen in the cup of your hands. But if it's a lucky fish, and that's an increasingly difficult thing to achieve today, it might grow to at least 6.5 feet and weigh over five hundred pounds. It might live forty years. The largest North Atlantic bluefin ever caught was pulled from the waters off Nova Scotia, weighing 1,497 pounds. It was twelve feet long.

Most people who know bluefins up close tend to remark on their beauty, their blue and silver colors, the gold wash across their sharply honed fins and spines, and the speed a whole school of them can muster. They are fish that swim just under the surface of the water, although they can dive to three hundred feet and can launch themselves into the air.

Their flesh is red, like the meat of a mammal. That's because their bodies have evolved a system of conserving the heat gener-ated by the large muscle mass through an intertwining of veins and arteries called the rete mirabile—the miraculous net—which protects the fish from the immediate chill of the surrounding water. The bluefins are endothermic, or warm-blooded, although they do not hold a constant temperature like mammals and birds do. What they can do is keep their bodies thirty or even forty degrees above the ambient temperature of the water, which gives them the freedom to penetrate much colder areas than fish without warming systems that are slowed by the chill. They move through water of varying temperatures with speed and an exceptional alertness, and this rare adaptation in a fish has allowed them to course the open oceans, both horizontally and vertically.

Our bluefin is the North Atlantic species, divided into two groups. If you draw a line to the left of the middle of the ocean straight down, starting at the level of Newfoundland to the Gulf of Mexico, you have their boundary, more or less. But they cross it constantly. The western population heads for the Gulf of Maine and up into the Gulf of St. Lawrence in spring, summer, and fall, but the fish also travel east, swimming back and forth across the ocean. Scientists have clocked them sprinting from the Gulf of Maine to the Spanish coast at 43 miles an hour. What distinguishes the groups is that one spawns around the Balearic Islands in the Mediterranean, the other in the Gulf of Mexico. In winter, our North Atlantic bluefins retreat to the Gulf of Mexico, where large schools circle in a spawning ritual, and all together, over a wide area, release thousands of eggs and sperm into the water.

How do you manage a fishery such as this? Not very well, is the easy answer. Since 2012, marine biologists have been working to bolster the diminished and endangered population of North Atlantic bluefins. It's a difficult science. They must figure out how to protect spawning areas, track the movements of adults, monitor the lives of the juvenile fish, and set international and enforceable policies.

But this isn't exclusively a bluefin tuna problem rather it's a general and increasingly fraught problem of how humans use the oceans. We depend on wild fish for 16 percent of the protein we eat worldwide; that's 88 million tons of fish we consume every year. Of these, bluefin tuna are one of the most sought after. Most wild fish species that humans consume exist on the verge of collapse, brought back by well-intentioned but anemic governmental restrictions, until it's decided to open a fishery once more, and it crashes.

What's going on? For one thing, over twenty million tons of fish are lost each year. Termed "by-catch," which means not the species the fisherman was after, purse seines, drift nets, and gill nets capture thousands of fish indiscriminately. Fishermen throw the rejects overboard, where they float away dead and dying. Hooks called "weak hooks" are allowed in long-lining when our North Atlantic bluefins are spawning in the Gulf of Mexico, permitting fishermen to go after swordfish. But they'll occasionally snag the tuna, and many of the spawners can't release themselves fast enough and die.

Those scientists who have dedicated themselves to marine conservation have proposed a number of ideas to rescue our oceans and the species that live within them from this downward spiral, among them large, inviolate marine sanctuaries; well-funded programs to develop fishing methods that target only the chosen species and only away from spawning areas; laws that prohibit all gear that would compromise habitat or cause prolonged suffering; and the phasing out of factory ships. These measures would help the bluefin species and others that are in decline around the world, and they would also initiate a different relationship we have with the oceans. Instead of pillage, it would be built on protection.

That bluefin skeleton hanging in the lobby of the science building has stayed with me. I think often about the majestic beauty and power of these animals, their long, swift peregrinations, the sight of a whole pack of them rushing just underwater. And I've thought about the students who put these bones together. Over months, as they learned about the life of this fish, they picked up the large and small bones from stainless trays, dipped them in glue, and fitted them into the places where they thought they belonged—along the spine, around the head, in the fins—crafting a testament to a wild life. That's not too far away from dipping a hand in paint to draw the body of a gazelle on a cave wall.

FOURTEEN

THE WHALES' GIFTS

IN APRIL AND MAY, whales swim into the Gulf of Maine, around our islands and close to shore. A few females have at their sides their precious calves. I am thinking not only of the journey up these coastal waters from our south Atlantic states and the Caribbean for right whales and humpbacks, but the whales' journey through time.

Of the first lives that crawled out of the sea and became land animals, a few eventually turned again to water, trading their legs for fins and flukes. The research suggests that small, deer-like animals that were waders and grazers may have become the leviathans we know. Although it took millions of years for this change to develop, I can't help but imagine a slim, long-legged animal, red-coated like the whitetails that feed on the ferns in my field in the summer mornings, wading, and the wading turning to paddling, and their beautiful heads going under and coming up, and going under again.

I am also a bit stuck on the fact that the nose traveled. It went from the front of the face onto the top of the head, where the splash guard protects the blowhole from a rush of water as the whale surfaces and breathes. And, like a footprint, biologists have found tiny bones of former femurs tucked within whale bodies that speak to the years that got them here.

This year 356 northern right whales are alive, and of those, nineteen are new calves, heading north with their mothers into the Gulf of Maine, around the Scotian Shelf to the Gulf of St. Lawrence, or up into the waters around Newfoundland and Labrador. The northern right whale is one of the most critically engendered whales in the world, and every calf counts.

Humpbacks live in all the oceans of the globe. Two separate populations travel either along the inshore of the Western Atlantic coast, heading north, or cross over from the waters of the Cape Verde Islands off Africa, and they both enter the Gulf of Maine. In 1985, humpback populations worldwide had dropped by 95 percent, due to whaling. Since then, the numbers are coming back, and here in the North Atlantic, humpback populations are listed as depleted, rather than endangered.

Oil for lamps and machinery, soap to keep us clean, margarine to spread on toast, baleen for whips and corsets, and ambergris from the guts of sperm whales to set the scents of expensive perfumes— as late as the 1900s, most people in the developed world couldn't get through the day without touching something made from the body of a whale. In those years approximately 270,000 whales were killed in the Northwest Atlantic alone, after hundreds of years of intense commercial whaling around the world. Whaling drew to a close in the Gulf of Maine in the 1890s because there were too few left to hunt, and every returning whale today reinvigorates a part of this huge but diminished body of water.

Now tour boats in the summer bays list from one side to the other as crowds rush from starboard to port to catch sight of a whale. I've seen people's joy at seeing them, and I share it. Despite these ecstatic sightings, perhaps the most precious gifts whales offer today are not glimpses of their private lives, but their fecal plumes, astonishing defecations that leave long, floating ribbons of buoyant fertilizer. These plumes drift at the water's surface with the floating plankton: the phytoplankton, which are minute algae, and zooplankton, species of tiny animals that move up and down in the top layer of the water column.

There, in the sunlight, the phytoplankton use the rich offerings of nitrogen, phosphorus, and iron in the whales' plumes to photosynthesize and grow. The zooplankton, such as krill and copepods, eat the phytoplankton. Schools of fish feed on the zooplankton, and then a right whale comes along and eats the copepods and a humpback comes along and eats the krill and the fish, and the whales rise to defecate as the cycle replenishes itself, beginning once more.

Scientists call the up-and-down movements in the water column of feeding whales "the whale pump." It creates a whisking effect, stirring more nutrients from the depths to the surface.

As the Gulf of Maine warms, the amount of phytoplankton drops because they depend on the oxygen that cold water carries. The more whales swimming into the Gulf present the phytoplankton with more of the nourishment they need, and they respond by producing oxygen. As phytoplankton, copepods, and krill diminish here, right whales and humpbacks swim elsewhere, seeking colder water and more abundant prey, and we are the poorer for it.

But for now, the whale plumes and pumps continue to feed the plankton that's in the Gulf, and the plankton eventually feed everyone right up the food chain. Not only do the whales nourish the foundational foods in this body of water, but the blooms of phytoplankton around the fecal plumes jolt our atmosphere with infusions of oxygen.

And here's a final gift from a whale: When it dies, it will sink to the bottom, carrying approximately thirty tons of sequestered CO_2 within it. Lying in the cold dark, it becomes food for the creatures who live in that peculiar habitat, and they strip it clean.

Joe Howlett died on July 10, 2017, from the blow of a right whale's flukes. He was 59 years old, a Canadian, and co-founder, in 2002, of the Campobello Whale Rescue Team. A man who loved whales, he never said no to an urgent call for help when a whale was spotted entangled in ropes from lobster or snow crab trap gear, dragging the weight of those traps and the heavy lines that can cinch around a whale's body as it tries to release itself.

He was also a lobsterman and crab fisherman. His friends report that he had a wicked sense of humor and a rare talent for the skill and courage required to brace against a rescue craft's bow and, with a specialized knife at the end of a long pole, reach out to cut the ropes around a wild animal that weighs as much as sixty tons, as it moves erratically and unhappily in the water.

"There's no better feeling than getting a whale untangled," a colleague of his said, "and I know how good he was feeling after cutting that whale clear."

Although the Campobello Recue crew usually operates in the Gulf of Maine, up into the Bay of Fundy, this entangled whale was spotted in the Gulf of St. Lawrence, and the team had driven north through New Brunswick to the town of Shippagan, taken a research vessel out into the water, and transferred to a Zodiac rescue craft that was faster.

Howlett had made the last cut, and the lines had begun to drop away from the whale. He turned then to the crew in the cabin of the research vessel behind him and held up a thumb for success. But the whale, in the water at the front of the zodiac, instead of swimming forward, suddenly began a quick and deep dive, turning to its side as it went down. Its flukes lifted out of the water and slapped down. Howlett was struck by enormous weight and force.

Speaking of the dangerous work of whale rescue, David Anthony, a member of the team, said, "If you don't get that strong high, that strong feeling from it, you'd probably not do it at all."

Joe Howlett believed that as a lobsterman and snow crab fisherman, he owed the whales this sort of rescue. He was good with ropes, good with the cutting tools, and he had a rare and focused energy about him. But new research has uncovered the troubling fact that many more whales are entangled and injured than the calls that send the rescuers out onto the water to do the same dangerous job again and again.

For instance, more than half of the humpbacks in the Gulf of Maine are scarred from previous entanglements. And the math and observational science indicate that at least 12 percent of all humpbacks that return here become entangled annually, and fewer than 10 percent of these are reported to rescuers.

Studies of northern right whale entanglement in the Gulf of Maine conclude that as many as 85 percent of them bear scars from entanglement, and 60 percent have been entangled more than once.

⌒‿⌒

Joe Howlett felt passionately about whales and he is mourned and missed by his family and friends.

What value should we assign to a whale's life? To, for instance, the pelagic food chain that whales support, and the oxygen that the phytoplankton produce supplemented by a single whale over its lifetime? What value to the carbon that a whale takes with it when it dies? Or to a girl on her first whale-watching trip seeing a humpback rise out of the water, an enormous presence, with crusts of barnacles on its head, and waves rolling off its back?

FIFTEEN

A WINTER GARDEN

I.

WHEN I LIVED IN PROSPECT HARBOR, my neighbors taught me that to live a good life at this tough and generous shore, a person needs to learn to love hard work and independence. That was in the last days of the boom time, before the busted fisheries.

Prospect Harbor is a coastal village in the municipality of Gouldsboro. The handful of small villages that make up the nearly 100 square miles of the municipality—45 of land and about 50 of water—has a population of 2,000 people, and most of the work that's done here has traditionally been done on the water. Not long ago, there were two canneries where women cut and packed fish caught by local fishermen in Frenchman Bay until the fish disappeared and the fishermen went wider and farther to find them. When I began cutting and packing herring at the cannery in Prospect Harbor, the catch was trucked in from Canada.

A year ago, in the heart of winter, I drove to South Gouldsboro and turned down the dirt road to Bunkers Cove, a small, tidy harbor about two miles from the cabin we used to live in when my kids were young. I came to see Sarah Redmond's new venture as the owner of one of those old canneries where she plans to process the seaweeds she farms out in the bay. This cannery was built in response to the war effort and went into production in 1943, cutting and packing alewives, mackerel, shad, herring, clams, and mussels to send overseas to the troops.

It isn't hard to see some of the history of overfishing in the story of the cannery that is now being rehabilitated to process organic seaweed instead of fish. It's called feeding down the food chain, in this case going from harvesting the abundant populations of fish in the Gulf of Maine to harvesting habitat. But you could also call it a project of healing. These are native seaweeds that Sarah grows. They benefit these coves, reinvigorating the health of the water and some of the wild systems that have been compromised.

Seaweed farms can be detrimental to the bays where they are sited if they are placed too tightly together, prohibiting the free flow of water, or if they introduce species that are not native, or overshadow other wildlife and the wild, free-growing seaweed beds. But if grown with care, as it seems to be done on this coast so far, over mud and sand bottoms where there is little, if any, interference with other sea life, seaweeds clean the water around them by gleaning the nutrients they need. They also create places for many small sea creatures such as carpella, or skeleton shrimp, to live. They absorb carbon, release oxygen, and when harvested are good for people to eat.

Farms such as Sarah's use the same ropes that lobster fishermen use for their traps—pot sink lines—made from polypropylene. No reports of entanglement with whales, dolphins, or seals have been noted at Maine seaweed farms yet. However, marine scientists have expressed concerns over the possibilities of lost or discarded ropes contributing to ocean trash, and a future of more, rather than fewer, marine mammal entanglements, already a serious problem within the lobster and crab fisheries.

Sarah suggests that perhaps because the mooring lines of small, inshore seaweed farms are anchored to the bottom, and fixed, they may make it easier for the mammals to see and avoid. Nonetheless, the issue is being closely monitored by animal welfare organizations and the Food and Agriculture Organization of the United Nations as large, offshore seaweed farms are being planned and financed with government monies on both sides of the North Atlantic. They will be vast sites to grow kelps on a massive level for biofuels and animal feed and fertilizers to be used in industrial land-based farming.

If ropes turn out to pose a danger, my anticipation is that Maine seaweed farmers will adjust their way of raising their crops to make their farms safe. Seaweed farming on this coast has been all about promoting environmentally healthy products, products that benefit, rather than harm, ocean life. It's an image these farmers stand by, work within, and wouldn't want to lose.

Sarah is young and skilled, hardworking and independent, and what I like best about her is that she's willing to try a new kind of harvest in these depleted waters. On an overcast day, she navigates her boat out into the bay to tend her garden, its mooring buoys bobbing in water that never gets much warmer in February than 29 degrees Fahrenheit. Here, to the north of Stave Island, her crop of skinny kelps, sugar kelps, dulse, nori, and Alaria twirl gracefully through changes of tide and weather.

After Sarah received her master's in marine biology from the University of Connecticut, she farmed seaweed for eight years, learning the trade. This new enterprise, however, is her first try at running a complete business. In the licensed patch of bay, she and a partner puzzle out together the best ways to raise their crops, which need cold, clean water to thrive. The seaweeds cling to the ropes, the horizontal long lines that hang six feet down. Each species requires specific light intensities. The trick is to have some of them throw a flickering shade onto others, but not too much, and to allow them all to absorb just the right amount of light they need, but not enough for the winter sun to scorch them.

At this tiny harbor, the old canning factory and its outbuildings are crowded close to the shore, a jumble of three buildings, and to one side, in the deep water, a neighbor's lobster pound is set in a broad half circle, marked off by pilings. Beyond it, a private dock reaches into the water. The dock that Sarah owns is on the other side of the cannery, where her Boston Whaler and harvest barge bob gently in the winter tide.

As we talked, Sarah described this new enterprise and how she planned to transform the old buildings into a state-of-the-art nursery to raise the tiny seaweed sporophytes, a processing room to clean and prepare the seaweeds, a room with a giant grinding mill that turns the crop to flour, and, she said a bit wistfully, she hopes to have a room set aside to teach organic seaweed farming to people who'd like to try it. Outside the buildings, she's found a spot to set up greenhouses to dry the crops.

What she has that reminds me of the best of the past is an eagerness to take on the work, and an ability to envision a different sort of future that she can bring to this harbor and this bay.

For the farmers who grow seaweeds in aquaculture sites in the Gulf of Maine, the season begins mid-September and can last into spring. When it closes, they haul in their ropes. The harvesters who cut wild edible seaweeds within the mainland bays and out around the islands pull on their wet suits and begin their season in April. Both wild seaweed cutting and seaweed farming that are specialized harvests of sea vegetables, minimally processed, are sold to companies and stores or directly to individuals. They're something Maine is beginning to be known for.

Almost all of them are small businesses in small coastal communities, most of them owned by the harvesters themselves. In Down East villages stricken by diminished fisheries, these bright entrepreneurial lights are doing well. The farmers and harvesters of edible seaweeds have learned from our past mistakes how to tend the wild carefully. No large industrial overreach has put the new ventures like Sarah's out of business. No corporate money from away has snuffed their homegrown independence—at least not yet.

II.

It's been a year since I wrote about Sarah's seaweed farm, and I'd like to know how she and her business are doing now. I give her a quick call and we set a date to meet.

As I drive across the bridge at Taunton Bay heading to Gouldsboro and the old cannery once more, the land begins to rise, and I see the sweep of Frenchman Bay. The waves in a mild fetch are flashing in the sunlight, and at the horizon lift the bare, rounded mountains of Acadia National Park.

The Frenchman whom the bay is named for is Samuel de Champlain. He sailed into this broad water full of coves and islands in 1604, encountering indigenous people at the shore as he mapped the coast for France. As I understand the history, Champlain's ship entered this water around Mount Desert in September, when the Wabanakis were gathering food at their summer encampments before heading inland for the winter. The story goes that the ship got stuck in an inlet, and the Wabanakis left off their chores to help the Europeans work it free.

What was going on beneath these small details of encounter was a first step of dramatic change: Champlain the mapmaker was initiating the process of European possession. His job was based on the Doctrine of Discovery, a series of papal bulls issued in the 15th century stating that Christians had the right to appropriate lands and the coastal water before them that were not inhabited by other Christians. These decrees, soon codified into law, gave Europeans both the legal and the moral backing to take land held by native people.

I drive down to the buildings of the old cannery, past the yurt Sarah's father built for her to live in on an uphill slope, its bright green panels a summer flourish in the soft gray monochrome of autumn by the ocean. I pass a new greenhouse.

The old buildings still want repair, but once I step inside the cannery, searching for Sarah, I find the place humming with seawater from taps that flow into large transparent vats in preparation for this year's seed production. In one vat, purple dulse swirls in the corkscrewing water. I stop to watch the dark fronds shaped a little bit like the paws of raccoons or the hands of children waving.

She's in the mill room, an immaculate space where she turns dried seaweeds into flours and powders and assorted seasonings. We walk outside and settle down for a talk at the picnic table set under a young maple by the shore. From where I sit, I can see again at the horizon the rounded mountains of Acadia. They are almost always visible from the land around this bay and Blue Hill Bay, but each angle emphasizes a different view, so they seem to be both solid and permanent, mutable and changing.

Things have stayed the same and also changed here at Sarah's business venture. She's named it Springtide Seaweed, and since I first came to talk with her, her long hours of work still revolve around these buildings and the stretch of waterfront before us. But her farming site has expanded to two areas in the bay now, totaling 55 acres. Despite the endless tasks of running an organic seaweed farm, she has not let go of her hope that this is the start of a cooperative effort by up-and-coming local seaweed farmers like herself.

"I want to train other people to do what we do," she tells me. "You build the organic aquaculture industry locally and you integrate it into the community with a shared infrastructure. My business partner and I have put together an organization we call The Organic Kelp Collaborative to create a network of trained people with the same growing standards. This way we can grow the seaweeds, build greenhouses together for drying them, and we're partners in the work. Here at the cannery we can mill all that seaweed into flour."

Though she still sells locally, most of her business is with national companies now that fold her flours and powders and seasonings into their own products. She believes that with a harvesting system and a network of local producers in place, most of the money that's made will stay here with the people in this Down East community.

"The opportunities are great," she says, leaning forward at the table and spreading her hands as if great were a quantity she could measure. But, she adds, the ocean is changing, and that means that our bays may start to lose some wild seaweed beds to warming water and to the spread of invasive species.

Wild seaweeds grow through the winter, as do the aquaculturally raised seaweeds. While the farming of seaweeds stops in the spring, the wild seaweeds, out in the bays as the summer wears on, begin to get fouled with organisms such as bryozoans, hydroids, and epiphytes that cling to the blades. No one knows how these native seaweed species will withstand the challenges of a changing climate and the resulting warming of the Gulf of Maine, or where the biggest changes may occur to the wild seaweed beds. Nor can we predict whether or not the warming trend will slow or speed up, or over time which species of seaweeds may adjust to it and thrive.

When you engage with underwater life and landscape, much of it is still unknown. For instance, rockweed species and *Ascophyllum nodosum* grow in the intertidal. You can walk to the shore to study them. They are not difficult to find because we see them beached when the tide withdraws, yet even the studies of these seaweeds, from which we've learned a great deal, present questions we haven't found the answers to.

"Seaweeds are a billion years old," Sarah says. "I don't think we're going to wipe everything out. I don't. But I do think interest in seaweed products is rising. As we become farmers, we can probably grow all the seaweed we'll need."

The crop, catching the bright winter sun, thrives into early spring, when it is harvested and the ropes are pulled out of the water. Then the water again becomes a space that's open. There's little overlap between the haul-out time at a seaweed farm and the setting out of lobster traps in the bays around here, and a few of the lobstermen and women in this community are interested in farming seaweeds seasonally with Sarah's help, before they start their summer work.

⌒

At the end of August of this year, local people took to the water in their fishing boats, sailboats, and kayaks, creating a beautiful theater of protest which they called the Save the Bay Flotilla. A hundred and twenty-five boats headed into Frenchman Bay, forming a line past the Bar Harbor pier.

They came because a Norwegian company has filed papers for permits to raise farmed salmon in 120 acres of this bay, in thirty net pens, each 150 feet wide. The company also plans to purchase the old sardine canning factory in Prospect Harbor to raise salmon for the pens, from eggs to smolts, and to process the harvested fish. They expect to produce 66 million pounds of farmed fish a year.

This project, if it is allowed by the state of Maine to proceed, would likely alter the boat traffic in the bay, the water quality of the bay, and underwater sea life. It might also affect the water quality of Blue Hill Bay. The two side-by-side bodies of water are not far apart, and each has a slow flushing capacity, which means that pollutants that leak into them tend to stay longer rather than to be pulled out and dispersed into open water quickly by the change of the tides. The fish pens would contain a system to remove fecal solids and to cycle and filter water from the pens that is then released, flushing four billion gallons of water daily into Frenchman Bay.

"What's going on here with the Norwegian company is economic colonization. Our opportunity," Sarah tells me, "lies with our people, our place. These big companies go where the wild resources are and they take them, and then when the resources run out, they leave. They move on.

"We're going to fight this. We're going to try to stop it. We're lucky because we have summer people in the area whose families go back for generations who are behind us, and we've got the Bar Harbor Chamber of Commerce, Acadia National Park, and Friends of Frenchman Bay. We've got a chance because for the first time it's the whole community together. If it were just me and the lobstermen, we'd be screwed."

The people who came to celebrate the protest at the Bar Harbor dock that August day held signs and cheered. They were noisy and celebratory and supportive.

I don't have any idea how to say "the more things change the more they remain the same" in Norwegian, but this salmon pen plan reminds me of Champlain's mapmaking. Salmon farming using floating ocean pens is an expensive and dirty and environmentally flawed business. It is in Norway, where citizens are beginning to speak out against the proliferation of pens along their coast, and it is in this country, despite some timely corrections. The company that hopes to build these pens calls itself American Aquafarms. It has a base in Portland and is run by people looking for opportunities to expand fish pens to this side of the Atlantic. Its directors expect to overcome the objections of local people, in part by offering jobs to this community, weakened by diminished fisheries.

When I first wrote about Sarah's new venture, I started by saying that what we were taught on this coast was to value hard work and independence. But I have come to believe that in order for coastal communities and their local enterprises to survive into tomorrow, what's required now is a commitment to work together to protect our bays, which will protect the future of these towns and villages.

Work and independence, still qualities of value, can be channeled into efforts to build a strong, managed commons. In such a place the harvesters themselves become the managers, drawing up rules for harvesting in the ecosystems in which they live and work that will preserve—and in some cases reestablish—the abundance of wild resources into the future. Ironically, it is probably the very people who have overharvested in the past who understand what's been lost, and a number of them are willing to work to fix what's broken.

A managed commons creates a collective independence and allows those who oversee it and abide by its rules a proprietary voice. It's also radically different from a system in which power and money do the talking, as they did that autumn long ago when a tall ship carried Champlain into a canoe culture.

It's late. I've just finished writing this story about Sarah's winter garden and the hope so many of us carry for a managed commons overseen by local people.

Out the windows of my house to the south, I can see the constellation of Delphinus, the dolphin, as it swims slowly west across the night sky. It's unseasonably warm tonight. There's no wind, which means that the water in the bay below the old cannery in South Gouldsboro is chucking softly against the pilings of the docks. Out farther, in the coves that fishermen have told Sarah were once the best places to catch the small, sweet-tasting boreal shrimp, a remnant population of them rises into the upper column of the water to feed on plankton. Out even farther, a right whale migrating down the coast with her growing calf rests in the water, and above them, a last flock of songbirds is flying south in the dark.

TIME ALONE

TIME ALONE

SIXTEEN

BECOMING A FLOCK

IN 1918, THE SPANISH INFLUENZA struck the tiny village of
Prospect Harbor in Down East Maine. Behind the closed doors of
the village houses members of families sickened and died. Others,
shut away against this monstrous and sudden curse, were terrified
that a neighbor might knock at the door asking for help, and they
would be forced to choose which was worse: saying no to someone
they had known all their lives, or exposing their family to the disease
that was ravaging the state. There were 45,000 cases reported in
Maine, and it is believed that many more people than that were
stricken.

I couldn't help but remember Miriam Colwell, a neighbor
and dear friend whom we met when we lived in Prospect Harbor.
She had lost her mother to the influenza soon after her birth, and
then her father died. She was raised by her grandfather, a widower.
Photographed by Paul Strand, posed in profile in black and white
and standing in front of a cedar-shingled shed, he was the post-
master of the village, a man of upright character and few words.
All her life Miriam, I believe, bore the scar of that time of loss. She
lived a wonderful, adventuresome life. And she became the post-
master of Prospect Harbor herself, like her grandfather. But she had
a door in her that was shut, and behind it, I imagine, was a residual
well of loneliness and grief.

In late March here at Morgan Bay, in the town of Surry, the nights are cold. The frog ponds freeze over with a thin glaze. The days, however, are longer, warmer, and the ponds melt back. Within these days and nights, the first birds from farther south return. A blast of robin song. A whispered warm-up from a purple finch. A song sparrow, from deep in the forsythia, strikes up a bar and lets it fade. Buffleheads, buoyant little ducks, are staging together out in the bay, getting ready to head inland, and the birds that have spent the winter alongside us, the nuthatches, juncos, and chickadees, tune up their noisy extravaganzas.

But this spring also initiates a different kind of season. We wake up to reports of illness and death. We go about making coffee. We tidy up. All together and all apart we take in the incomprehensible news of our own species and begin our solitary hours.

My house sits at the end of a long driveway in the woods with a field in front, on a road where neighbors, for years, have gathered for picnics, a St. Patrick's Day party, or an especially good night to see the stars. This neighborhood may be as many others are, but we who live here believe it's special. Most of us came to Maine in the '70s—moving away from urban centers. We left for different reasons, but one we had in common is we thought with more space around us, more room to breathe, we could construct our lives and bring up our children in ways that were better than the generations before us. I think that all generations believe that they can do better and, of course, we succeed, but we also fail in a number of ways.

What held us together was a love of the land we were living on and the bay we lived by. We built small homes and raised big gardens and made careers for ourselves. Some of us became close friends, sharing our lives, but all of us seem to understand that a neighborhood is something to value, and we tend to, most of the time, treat each other with care. We also agree about many of the issues of the day, which include our need to protect what is left of what we have here, and to learn how these wild systems around us work.

Two weeks ago, in the middle of the pandemic, we initiated the Social Distancing Bird Club. We're a baker's dozen, and we report what we see by e-mail, a back and forth that has become a lively celebration not only of what it is to be neighbors in this scouring time, but a celebration of wild birds. This club of ours opens the door that the pandemic had closed between us, like the closed doors in the time of the Spanish flu.

No matter how much any one of us knows or doesn't know about bird identification, it doesn't matter, because we puzzle out together over the Internet the songs, sightings, and the behaviors we encounter on our walks or what we see from the windows of our homes. One of us heard a ruffed grouse drumming in the woods yesterday. A few have seen bluebirds. No warblers yet. No vireos. No hermit thrushes or tree swallows. No hummingbirds or common terns. Spring is still to come.

Birds are a way into the world outside ourselves. Here, you can look out your windows or go into the woods and sit down quietly, and soon, not always, but often, a bird or two will move into your line of sight, into your range of hearing, going about its life, a life that seems particularly intense and quick and alert. And you stand or sit and watch.

The variety of birds in the world, the particular lives they live by season and weather and light and darkness, is more than most of us will ever know. But we know something, and species by species we learn, and the birds around us become neighbors, and our neighborhood deepens. We become, through this wild intimacy, protectors, refusing to lose what we have grown to care for. In our case, it's by working to protect what's left of the land around us.

When I was first learning about wild birds, I had to learn to focus my attention, to practice patience, and to let the birds take their own good time doing what they do. That's how one becomes a birder. And a witness. Becoming a witness changes how you feel about what you see and hear. It happens when a detail from a bird's life lives on in your imagination. You choose to carry it for the spark of joy it offers.

The wild birds of Canada and the United States are having their own pandemic as we have ours. Theirs has gone on longer. Individuals lost to pesticide poisoning, habitat destruction, and climate change in the last fifty years number close to three billion. The number is stunning.

In our neighborhood in these damp, changeable days of late March turning into April, we're clear about some things. One is simply that we're all in this together, the birds and ourselves. We don't have to figure out what use a robin or a grouse is to our small community. They owe us nothing. We, on the other hand, owe them quite a bit.

Perhaps, when we resume our lives, we won't forget this cloistered time when we stood at our windows more than we used to or sat down on a stump in the woods by ourselves and saw life go on despite crushing losses, despite the fear. We saw mating chases through the branches of the softwoods and a bit of nest building as a mourning dove and a dark-eyed junco searched for materials, the female dove for light, thin sticks, the female junco for pliant last year's grasses. We watched the blue jays stream through in raucous bands, beautiful and thuggish, and a Cooper's hawk shoot across the yard, which made everyone stop, go still.

This morning a black-capped chickadee pair is checking out the birdhouse by the upper frog pond. I'll add them to the e-mail thread of the day very soon—but for now, I'll watch.

SEVENTEEN

HAPPY, HAPPY HOURS

IN THE 17TH CENTURY John Josselyn traveled from England to New England to study the wildlife—especially the plants—of the New World. His was the first detailed and enduring record of the natural history of wild Maine. Approximately two centuries later, in 1895, the Josselyn Botanical Society was formed at the Portland Museum of Natural History. Named in his honor, with botanist and artist Kate Furbish as one of its founders and one of its first vice presidents, it slowly changed the way we see the wildflowers we encounter today.

Kate Furbish was sixty-one years old by then, already well known for her botanical illustrations of Maine wildflowers, a woman of small stature, sharp features, and a rather invincible, perhaps even pugnacious nature. She could be charming, but she was tough, a single woman all her life, living in the house she grew up in, and painting the flowers she collected at a small table in the corner of her bedroom.

I am sitting at my kitchen table, with a fine-tipped Sharpie in hand, trying to conjure onto a piece of drawing paper the dry winter stalk and seed head of a monarda I've set in a canning jar. It's what's left of a bee-balm flower. This conjuring isn't easy. My first try looked like Oscar the Grouch from behind. The more I stare at the seed head, the more I notice the smallest of details, and the more complicated and astonishing this ordinary summer leftover becomes.

It's likely I would not be doing this if the coronavirus hadn't turned me into a full-time hermit, and if I hadn't recently come across two books highlighting Kate Furbish's watercolors of Maine wildflowers. She saw what my eyes have blurred for years. Now, I am trying to see as she did. My friends are all at a remove, as are my kids and grandkids. We talk on the phone, we Zoom, but we are behind the walls of our homes, in enclosures that we hope will keep us safe. And who knows what the future will bring?

I am taken by Kate Furbish's passion and her extraordinary talent. Although in photographs she looks strait-laced and sober, a Victorian you might want to approach with some caution, the truth seems to have been that the time she spent with her flower books in Maine's woods, alone exploring along its lakes and river-banks, seeking the wildflowers that she wanted to take home and paint, kept her in an almost constant state of exhilaration. "Called 'crazy,' a 'fool' this is the way my work has been done," she wrote, "the flowers being my only society and the manuals the only literature for months together. Happy, happy hours!"

I'm on to the seedpod of a swamp milkweed. I grew it last summer in a patch of this particular species and checked every morning for the monarch caterpillars that hatched from eggs a butterfly had laid on the leaves, and then I watched the caterpillars eat the leaves, growing larger by each day, until they disappeared to change into pupae. The deer came and ate the plants almost to the ground. Deer aren't supposed to like milkweed, but this beautiful stalk with its lovely pointed seed heads and striated tips is all I have left.

I find that shadow and light have everything to do with the illusion of making something seem real on paper. The job seems to be that to get a three-dimensional sense of a milkweed pod, you have to make it look as if it's turning at the tip, so that you catch a glimpse of its underside, and you need to make sure that the stalk looks like more than two parallel lines down the page. The chaotic fluff and the closely packed arrangement of the seeds are especially difficult, and so is the way the seeds tuck so neatly into the belly of the dry pod.

Kate Furbish had been, to paraphrase Jane Austen, a young woman of few prospects. Like Austen, she never married, but was sustained by the attentions and finances of her comfortable middle-class family. There were 59 years between Austen's birth and Furbish's; nonetheless, in the 18th and 19th centuries in which they lived, many women in like circumstances kept to the edges of robust family life, dim shadows by the hearth. But some didn't. Some were talented and rather fierce. Both Austen and Furbish managed to create disciplined, complex lives and to send into the world outside their homes their extraordinary work.

Furbish's watercolors shine with precision in both structure and color. My favorites are her rendering of red maple flowers and her delicate portrait of bloodroot. I have also found her painting of a monarda, spare and delicate and alive, an individual flower poised like a dancer on a wide expanse of white paper.

Today I am struggling with a small branch I snipped from my shadbush, with its tight shields of leaf and flower buds that are waiting through the winter to burst open in spring. On these cold days, I spend a surprising amount of time at the kitchen table with these parts of the wild world—up close—full of edges and textures and subdued color.

The Josselyn Botanical Society has continued ever since its inception. Its membership has grown, but its influence is far wider, because members go out into their communities and teach the rest of us. Although at first it may have seemed to the general public only a gathering of a peculiar bunch of people who liked to slog into shaggy damp places together, it has become a force that prompts us to understand the value of native plants where we live. Not only do we learn about protecting them, but we learn to identify them and know their history.

In his great elegy, Thomas Gray wrote "Full many a flower is born to blush unseen / And waste its sweetness on the desert air." I think Furbish would take issue with those lines. I think she might shake her head and say, quite plainly, that flowers aren't wasted because human eyes don't rest on them. That their value is not certified by our gaze. A bee's attention is enough. Or a butterfly's. Whether we see them or not, we are surrounded by gorgeous, valiant adaptations to living a full life.

Both Austen and Furbish knew how to live their lives and how to see: one into the hearts and follies of her neighbors, the other into the stems and leaves, roots and blooms of Maine wildflowers. These two women wasted nothing. And my guess is they rarely blushed.

EIGHTEEN
INTERESTING TIMES

"MAY YOU LIVE IN INTERESTING TIMES" is purported to be a Chinese curse, but no one has pinned down its true origin. It could be from anywhere. Or everywhere.

Today as I write this, there's not a doubt that here, and across the world, we've tripped into a deep fissure, a dark shaft of interesting times. Perhaps when you read this we will have crawled up and out, and stand in light-hearted air, free of COVID and wildfires and all the other terrible news.

If you are not sick or tending others who are, staying home is hard. Most of us squander time, but if we let it, this self-imposed journey into stillness, this hermitage, can offer space to think and create—to wander imaginatively—to rediscover some things that we find make us happy. But to do this we've got to tamp down fears that flare like the wildfires.

What have you done with these hours? What have I done with them? Yesterday, after work, I climbed the attic stairs and pulled vinyl records out of a stack I hadn't touched for years, their covers delivering a bold whiff of dust and mold. I carried them down and played them on the phonograph, the volume loud. Tchaikovsky, Mozart, Bach. They had belonged to my mother. I remembered this music she loved drifting out the open windows of our family house in summers a long time ago.

In these most interesting of times, we call our children, we call sisters and brothers and friends. We call the people who are frail and who need our voices to tell them that we care, that we haven't forgotten them. And they call us. Back and forth, it becomes a weave of familiar, beloved voices. But, in truth, it is a time of quiet and retreat.

I've spent a good part of the evenings recently rereading Jane Austen's *Emma*. I need Austen's wit, her gimlet eye. I need her to remind me to be kind to others, perhaps especially at this distance. Emma's journey to kindness makes for a long book, and I, like so many others, wait for Mr. Knightley's slap-down: "Poorly done, Emma!"

I've also been tramping out into the yard from the raised beds to the frog ponds and back, through the stands of red maples and white pines. There are invasive plants to uproot and cut down: the infuriating knotweeds, the grasping tangles of bittersweet, the sprawling persistent snags of Russian olive. And there are plants that are still dormant to be nurtured and tended: blue flags and pickerelweeds in the pond shallows, wild bergamots, violets, primroses, goldenrods across the yard and field. The virgin bower will leaf out. The dandelions will spread a carpet of early pollen for the bees across the grass. Spring is barely here—winter barely gone.

Back to the kitchen table, where I've taped together pieces of paper to map this place, I block in a new milkweed bed, a new herb plot, scribble notes about the future of the yard as if this were the most urgent of all endeavors, as if my yard were the world. Which it is in a sense. All of us on this back road seem to be in agreement that our private spaces are one long stretch of habitat. We tuck in native plants wherever we can. We let our fields grow up. We like to make sure there are things here that will sustain species other than our own—and this work gives us comfort. It's a burst of good health.

But yesterday, at dusk, I was wrung out. I could not wrench from the ground one more bittersweet root. Rather, I went and lay down by the lower frog pond and looked up at the sky as clouds shaped like a school of small fish swam west. From back in the trees, a first male robin delivered a blast of territorial singing and a wood frog piped up from the water as I lay within this singing and the ebbing light.

NINETEEN

POOR JOANNA

AT THE END OF THE SAILING ERA, after the Civil War, the coast of Maine became a quieter place. We'd lost our international shipping and shipbuilding grandeur, and the state had lost soldiers who'd gone to fight in the war. Coastal villages were now places where the everyday lives of women suddenly came to the fore. Those voices were always there, of course, but now they filled an empty space.

When I think of this, I remember in Eudora Welty's *One Writer's Beginnings* that she wrote of how she as a child would often play under the kitchen table in her family home as the neighborhood women gathered to drink tea in the afternoon, and those voices, those turns of speech, that weave of storytelling and gossip became her first lesson in language. Like Welty's women drinking tea, Sarah Orne Jewett's *Country of the Pointed Firs* is told mostly through the voices of the women in the fictional town of Dunnet Landing.

So much of early Maine storytelling is about ridge runners and logging camps, fighting the British and the tribes for control of the land, and the perils of the ocean—these were men's stories. Jewett's writing reflects a period where things were subdued, intimate, reflective.

When I first moved to Maine, and lived not far from the shore, I read *Country of the Pointed Firs*. I read it by kerosene light at the kitchen table of our cabin outside of Prospect Harbor a year after we'd arrived because I wanted to know about the place we'd come to. As a late 20th-century reader, I am sure I didn't read it as Jewett's contemporaries did. For me it was a lesson in a period of small-town culture, in voice, in language, and in the ways of courtesy that were different from the place I'd come from. It taught me to tone down my own voice, and to listen. Although it spoke to a time long past, I found it helpful. Jewett showed me something of the manner and wit of my neighbors of this traditional small Down East town.

Within her story of intricate and complicated village life is another story of extreme solitude. It's about a woman named Joanna, who, when deceived by her lover, sets sail for Shell Heap Island and never returns, a peculiar response to a man whom Jewett says through one of her characters was a "shifty-eyed, coaxing sort of man." But Joanna decided that the betrayal caused such a storm of wrath and shame and guilt inside her, she was done with life in the village world.

I think everyone carries within themselves the sense of an island, a part of themselves that is separate from the whole. I find that what I took from Joanna's story all those years ago was not her hurt, but her strange courage. What I carried in those years of raising children, tending a big garden, and trying to make ends meet was the story of the woman who went away to live by herself. My life was too busy, and sometimes, driving from one place to another, I'd glance out across the bay to an island set against the horizon and remember Joanna and her tidy little garden; her spare, neat cabin; and her solitary walks around the strict perimeters of her entire world. Not that I wanted the same for myself forever, but maybe a day or two, maybe a week, and then to return to those I loved, to the life I loved.

Other women who read Jewett's book told me they felt the same. Joanna may have been odd, but that oddness spoke to us. She'd given up on love, but those of us, young women who had moved here as I had and were learning how to live in a brand-new place, working hard at roles we felt we needed to fill, and fill well, hadn't given up on love—we just needed a few breaks.

What I think I see, rereading the story today, is that the people of the mainland, the people who cared about Joanna, thought of her as we had. I believe she became a template for a secret part of themselves that sometimes dreamed of loosening the bonds of civic life and all its big and small responsibilities, to go away and live alone in a place they glimpsed when out fishing or sailing down the coast. In the book, the women of the village discuss Joanna over their knitting. Couples, tucking in for the night in a darkness roaring with wind and snow, worry about her. She's out there in that chaos, lying on her cot, or gazing out the window at pure night. Maybe this time, she'll return to them. But she never does.

They left her gifts at the island cove: food from mainland farms, some laying hens and chicks to raise, and other practical things, life-saving things. When they sailed by again, they'd see she'd picked up whatever they had set there. I think of these offerings and her silent acceptance of them as a conversation between the contrary aspects of who we are as individual people. On the mainland, Joanna might have married, settled in, become much like everyone else: hard-working and neighborly. Instead she became a beacon, streaming a light across the water to the main, reminding her townsfolk that each of us carries a particular and complicated fire within.

The narrator, who has heard about Joanna's life from two of the townspeople, travels to the island and walks it alone to find Joanna's gravestone, years after her death. The cabin is gone, the garden has grown up, subsumed by wild grass and sedge. Joanna's island had become a pilgrimage for many who thought that their own lives might reflect something of hers, and the village gently took her story for its own, enfolding it into all the other stories it told about itself, as if she'd never left.

TWENTY

TIME ALONE

SOMETIMES A PAINTING WILL lodge in your mind. You carry the image around and your days filter their hours through it, as if it were a place you might have lived in a long time ago, and the uncertain memory of it stays for a while, a ghost-like presence, familiar but also at a distance, before it eventually fades.

These last days, the narrative of my life has been touched by Winslow Homer's *The Artist's Studio in an Afternoon Fog*. You can find it on the Web or in a book of his oil paintings, when, in his last years, he set out to paint the sea from his place on Prout's Neck. Who would ever set out to paint the sea, especially here in Maine? How could anyone get it right? Well, Homer did.

Those of us who live on this coast know something about the magic of water. We've seen how it comes in as a building tide, lifting the knotted wrack so that their blades spread out and wave like trees in the wind. We know the withdrawing tide leaves pools in the mud and cobble of dead low, where mummichog schools swim, awaiting the water's return. We've seen our high-tide bays as flat as mirrors, and the terns fishing above them, and we've seen them wild in a storm and watched in a snow squall the white flakes vanish into the dark uneasy waves. The colors of our home bays always shift, and some of the blues and greens, the off-whites and the grays we have no names for.

Homer's canvas that has lived with me these days has none of his famous breaking waves. It is still, except for a small ruffle of water along the far ledge and a glint of water pooling on the rocks up close. An oil painting in browns, dense black, and silvery whites, it was made in 1894, after he had decided to spend most of his time on this stretch of the coast and commissioned a stable by the shore to be rebuilt as a studio where he could keep to himself and work.

The sun burning into the fog in the painting creates a light that seems crepuscular. It looks like evening, but it's one of those middays when warm air moves across the cold surface of the Gulf and hits a dew point, dropping a gauzy curtain along the shore. You, the viewer, see his studio through this veil of fog, ghost-like, and beyond the studio, the family home.

What I see in the painting now is an echo of the time we're going through. The artist's studio is poised at the land's edge, bearing witness to a vast and complicated and unpredictable sea. To some extent we're all standing like that studio: far apart, and on the edge, watching a world that is very beautiful and dangerous.

The painter has put himself at a distance, looking back at his studio covered in this protective fog. That is a double vision, the sort that many of us are feeling as we live through this COVID crisis and climate change. We see ourselves not only within these catastrophes, but often also outside them, staring at the utter unraveling around us with a sense of incredulity.

I'd have liked to be Homer looking back at his studio in the fog, that steady, anchored building that looks like it could never be blown away, and inside I'd imagine myself patiently layering paint, patiently, slowly, building up a canvas. He's busy turning paint into waves and ledge and sky because that's the life he's given himself. He's alone in one of the most challenging ways there is to be alone, for he's working at a vision, making the choices of brushstroke and color, turning something as restless as the sea, as blunt and shapely as the rocks, as complex as the sky, into paint.

Homer was a private man by temperament. When at work, he was sharp-tongued and formidable in his insistence on being by himself. Legend has it that he hoisted a flag up the studio flag-pole when he wanted lunch delivered and passed the plates out a window to his hired man when done. When he was at work, which was most of the time, he thrived in isolation and silence, except for the sounds of the ocean seeping in through the windows.

I think of *The Artist's Studio in an Afternoon Fog* as I drive past my neighbors' oddly subdued homes to shop—which I do quickly, masked, with many squirts of hand sanitizer when I reach the safety of the car again. Most of us are trying to make out of this quiet and more solitary time than we're used to something good, something hopeful. It's not easy.

There is a difference between being told to stay home to stay safe and doing what Homer did in those years at the shore, which was to choose to turn away from the human world to see if he could make something that told the truth and would last. Living in a different sort of alone time now, it seems to me he did just that.

TWENTY-ONE

THE MAP

MY MOTHER SENT ME a map in the mail, glued to a sheet of thin cardboard and folded into a big manila envelope. She had paper-clipped a note to it, telling me that this was the first special present she had ever bought for herself, and she had found it in a shop that sold antique books and other curiosities in New York when she was a senior at George Washington Academy in Washington Heights. It was, she wrote, a copy of Henry David Thoreau's hand-drawn map he had made of his walks on Cape Cod in the mid-1800s, the one she'd taken with her and followed to Orleans and on to Province-town. She wanted me to have it.

It was April. I was a senior in college, struggling to finish a thesis. I opened the envelope and drew out the map with its glossed and yellowed paper, the shadows of stains upon it, the uptilt of the arm of the Cape with its bent elbow, and Thoreau's tight, faded scribble alongside the dark lines marking his route, shadowed by pencil lines of her own walking trip that my mother had drawn lightly over the original. It was something earnest and personal, and it had more to do with my mother's journey than with Thoreau's, I suspected, and what she had dared long ago.

She sent it because she thought I was about to embark on a journey myself, she wrote in the letter that followed, and she wanted me to see and to own a bit of hers. But I had no plans for a journey. A year before, I had studied at the University of Madrid. More than a little lost back in this country, I hadn't really come home yet. I slid the map in the envelope it came in and stuffed it into a bureau drawer in my cramped, chaotic dorm room.

Today as I put together the parts I remember of my mother's walking trip, I am reminded that my mother and father were alive during the First World War as very young children, and lived through the 1918 flu, the Great Depression, and the Second World War. They never framed their own narratives as exceptionally bleak, although my father's uncle did fight with the Australian army at Gallipoli. Yet, when I look back, I see that my mother's journey across the Cape must have come out of a long season of loss, a will to leave it behind and to set out for something new. My way back to her story of her hike on the Cape is to stitch the fragments that I remember into a whole that I am not sure adheres to all the facts, and she is not here to ask. But I have the handful of things my memory has held on to. They will have to be story enough.

Why do this now? COVID-19 has brought changes to our lives. One of them is the inward space it has offered some of us that is quieter and more expansive than our usual days allow. Into them flow memories of faces and voices and the stories that have been tucked away. They surge like a stream when a jam is breached, carrying away old leaves and branches, rolling pebbles forward into side pools, clearing the way for water. The memories have the space now to come alive.

I am also revisiting Thoreau's book *Cape Cod* because my mother's story begins with his. Thoreau visited the Cape three times, in 1849, 1850, and 1855, taking a coach from his hometown of Concord to the coast. As I reread the collection of essays about these visits, published after his death in 1862, I don't remember my mother talking about them. But she must have. I know she read *Walden*—more than read it, for I believe she wanted, when she was young, and in her own way, to live by it. She, of all people I have known and loved, needed that beat of a different drum. And as a very young woman, the drummer she chose was the writer himself, whose examined life she worked to reflect in her own.

Thoreau's book starts with the wreck of the *St. John*, a ship bringing the Irish from the famine to the new world in 1849. Those ships were called coffin ships because so many immigrants died on the trip across. Much like refugees today, the Irish were seeking safe haven. In his journals, Thoreau's reactions to the influx of poor Irish are mixed. As much as he complained about them, he also praised their virtues and courage. In a short passage in the book, he writes of a young Irish boy going to school in rags, a hungry child, whose face lit up with joy at the adventure of schooling. Quietly, Thoreau helped both the child and his family.

His writing in this first chapter of *Cape Cod* is not the place to first meet him. No two chairs for friendship, three for society here. No bluebirds flitting across the pond carrying the sky on their backs. It's a cold, impersonal description of the water's chaos and the dead sprawled along the beach for miles at the edge of the roaring tide: bodies half buried in sand, lost shoes, hunks of the ship, tatters of clothing. It shocks a reader—this reader and others—not for his choosing to write about it, but for his seemingly easy acceptance of its horror.

Who is this man we thought we knew? And why did he go out of his way to walk that calamitous beach? Cohasset, the town where it took place, isn't even on the Cape, but over sixty miles northeast of it.

The sea was too rough to take the ferry across to the Cape, he explains, and so he went to visit the tragedy for himself. I believe he had to see it. The relentless cataloguing of the wreckage, human and otherwise, set off against the calm men and boys along that stretch of sand collecting seaweed for their fields and gardens, forking it into wagons pulled by their farm horses, is a searing trope of opposites. It offers a clue to why he was there. The scene is reminiscent of W. H. Auden's image in the poem "Musee des Beaux Arts" of the torturer's horse rubbing its backside against a tree: two things going on at once, close together and a world apart. Life continues in the midst of horror. The gardens and fields need compost. That itch needs scratching. Alongside catastrophe and cruelty continues the quotidian of the day at hand. That's what Thoreau was working to accept.

I believe that my mother would have understood this emotional undercurrent, this stark punishing scene of Thoreau's, because she may have intuited that he was forcing himself to take another long, unblinking look at death up close. His life had been savaged by it. He wrote it cold because he had lived it hot.

In 1842, he lost his beloved brother and closest friend, John, to lockjaw, holding him as he convulsed and died in his arms. Afterward, Thoreau was oddly passive toward everyone around him, a silent nonpresence for days. Then he came down with the symptoms of lockjaw himself. He didn't have tetanus. A nearly fatal grief was locked inside him, until it slowly drained away. In Cohasset, already anticipating that his tubercular lungs would never heal, seven years after his brother's death and seven years before his own, he needed to understand death in the midst of relentless, ongoing life. And that, to a point, is one of the things the book is about.

The wreck of the *St. John* is a portal that readers must pass through to gain the rest of what Thoreau has to tell. It's grim, but it leads to what he accomplished after returning over and over to the Cape: a certain peace. An acceptance of what seems unacceptable. The book becomes, eventually, a narrative of the wise heart, allowing joy and humor and irony in. When he read parts of it, as he wrote it, at the Concord Lyceum, he had the audience in tears—of laughter. I believe that my mother chose the Cape as Thoreau did. It was a place to discover and return to, a teacher of essential things.

My mother's grandfather Patrick Ryan, who would later open Ryan's Oyster and Chop Houses in New York City, came over on a ship like the *St. John* a few years after the miasma of the famine had subsided and his family could risk the trip from the County Mayo coast to the city of Limerick where the transatlantic sailing ships were moored. He was a young boy then, holding on to his father's hand, and this was his path to a new life.

When my mother set out on her hike across the Cape, she was eighteen. Her father, Patrick, named after his father, had died two years before. I have a photo of him in a bowler hat, a stiff white collar, a formal jacket, and a nice tie. His head is slightly cocked to the side, as if he had a sense of humor and felt a bit jaunty— or maybe a bit foolish—having this rather formal portrait taken. Despite the head tilt, if you look closer, his eyes seem tired, a little sad. He was blue eyed, dark haired, with a narrow face, a narrow chin. I have another photo of him with my mother as a child, taken somewhere outside in the sun. His shirtsleeves are rolled up and he is smiling. He's a handsome young father.

He died in 1927 at the age of 38. Diagnosed with esophageal cancer, in this case brought on most likely by alcohol, he survived an operation that today seems unthinkable: surgeons inserted an opening directly, as I understand it, into his stomach, circumventing, or perhaps removing, what was left of the esophagus. His food was ground fine, mixed with warm water, and dripped through a funnel set into the hole above his navel.

Patrick had played the piano, learning songs by ear, and accompanying himself in a strong tenor. For a time, he worked with his father in real estate, and they made comfortable money, enough to afford roadsters and long vacations. Then there seems to have been a slow economic slide. I don't know why, exactly. But I do know that Patrick became an occasional binge drinker. He would disappear for a few days, then turn up, often bringing a peace offering for my mother, a puppy or a kitten he'd found on the street, which my grandmother never let her keep. Despite all this, he was a man of some charm and a quick grace, qualities my mother inherited. During his final months she tended him after school let out, feeding him through the funnel as he lay on the living room couch. Her mother, for the first time in her life, went out of the apartment to work, finding a job in a dress shop.

What is surprising to me is that my mother, whose name was Dorothy, came out of the family I describe: an insular, country-raised mother of little education; a handsome father who brought her a bit of enchantment, a lot of sorrow. She had a beautiful face from childhood on through much of her life. It wasn't an impersonal beauty, nor was there artifice to it. She had, quite simply, the gift of elegant, classic features; a perfect nose; and blue eyes that looked directly at you, not in a piercing fashion, but in a patient and hopeful one. Perhaps the more interesting thing is that in the time I am describing, she loved school and her teachers, her introduction to literature, serious music, art, modern dance, the theater. Where did this rarified appetite come from? Through all the hazards of her growing up and for the rest of her life, these would be her comfort and delight.

Dedicated teachers helped her fill out an application for Sarah Lawrence in Yonkers, where she won a full scholarship before her high school graduation in the spring of 1929. When she visited the campus, however, she saw how different from herself the girls appeared to be, with their expensive clothes and casual manner. She had neither the manner nor the clothes. In August, she turned down her place at the college and took a job. Then October arrived, the banks collapsed, the world fell apart for those college girls, for her frightened mother, for the entire city around them. My mother lost her job, packed up Thoreau's map, and left for the Cape.

When Thoreau reaches the Cape, which he calls "a wild rank place, and there is no flattery in it," he becomes a well-versed travel writer, witty, clever, offering his readers an 1850s landscape foreign to most of them. For them at that time, the Cape was a frontier, full of what was left of the untethered wild. It was also a place of human folly and expertise, accident and exuberant life, as well as death and ruin. The ocean was the giver and taker of godlike extremes, hammering against that arm of sand he walked across, scraping the beach away and tossing it up somewhere else. Between the water and the waves and the wind, the place was deafening. It forced people along the beach to shout at each other to be heard and, as often as not, their words drowned before they ever reached another's ear. It was monotonous as well, with too much sand, too much rain, too many waves, and the human inhabitants wrinkled and worn and patched, their homes hunkered down against the wind. But it drew him.

The Cape would have been an intriguing curiosity to those who kept house in Concord, that inland town by the river, well established, intellectually robust, a center of New England culture and thought, including, of course, Transcendentalism. Thoreau took his personal brand of Transcendentalism beyond the confines of Concord, testing it at Maine's Katahdin, the sacred mountain of the Penobscots, and along the narrow strip of shore bordering the ocean at the Cape.

Sometimes the sun broke through the fog and the bogs shimmered with light. Sometimes the waves, cresting far offshore and racing inland, crossed under a stab of sunlight and became blue then green, then foam white. He discovered that in summer there were camp meetings where long-winded preachers of questionable talent competed against the ocean's roar. Thoreau found the preaching one could live by in the ocean's voice, he tells us, and in the sound of the spray and the wind.

For some readers, there is far too much talk of sand in the book. For my taste, it's worth the price to be present at the Wellfleet oysterman's house for a breakfast one would never want to repeat, and to learn how the 19th-century lighthouse keepers tended their lanterns, checking the wicks at night and the mirrors that projected those lights, and the window glass that had to be constantly polished to keep the beam true, and all the curious and deep knowledge these isolated keepers shared in bits and pieces with Thoreau. He was a writer who was interested in those bits and pieces of the world and how they fit together.

He advised his readers in *Walden* to beware of all enterprises that require new clothes, and that was fine for my mother. She had few new clothes. She did buy hiking boots and a large rucksack. She borrowed a pair of lederhosen from a friend and took along two pairs of black cotton leggings to wear under them, and, I assume, a copy of *Cape Cod*. That was about it. She went by train and bus to Dennis, and crossed over by foot as Thoreau had done on one of the walks he took from the bay side to the ocean. The Cape in her time was not the same as in Thoreau's, of course. Eighty years had passed. Still dominated by fishing boats and fishermen, as Thoreau had described, it was more settled, a place of summer theater, comfortable rooms for let in village homes, and simple meals. It hadn't, however, lost its edge. Still dangerous at the shore, it shifted relentlessly between life-giving excess and the ocean's capacity to do harm, a setting in which both Thoreau and my mother found some truth of the world before them that they could live by.

One of the more peculiar episodes of Thoreau's journeys is when a local farmer carried him over a bog pond on his shoulders. This is the portaging of a grown man clutching a daypack. With doleful eyes and a shaggy beard, he's perched up on the shoulders of a Cape Cod farmer, and I can't quite bring myself to see it. It's easier to imagine the time he leaned against the shingles on the side of the

Wellfleet oysterman's house and vomited up a surf clam he had cooked for himself on the beach for lunch.

The business of cultivating cranberries on the Cape began in 1816 when a Revolutionary War captain began experimenting with raising the berries in the bog lands he owned. By the time Thoreau took his walks, it was an industry in its infancy. He doesn't mention that the bog he was being carried across was a cranberry bog, and he may not have encountered one. My mother, however, did.

"I must have followed the map too closely," she told me. She had set out to wade across a bog, thinking it was shallow enough. But in October, the cranberry holdings were diked and flooded. They were at their deepest then, as the ripe fruits detach from their stems and float toward harvest. My mother turned back when the water reached her waist, and struggled to the bank, climbing up a small rise of sand. There she unbuttoned and stepped out of the lederhosen, peeled off her drenched stockings, squeezed the water out of them, and lay in her underpants in the hot autumn sun, falling asleep as her clothes dried.

She was alone and so young. I worry, even as I write this, at how unprotected she was, as I did when she first told me. But she's all right. As a matter of fact, she's fine. I remind myself, as I think of her lovely face, asleep, on that sandy rise, so far away from anything but ocean and scrub pines, cranberries and sand, that she will come back to the Cape some years later, to the playhouse in Dennis, as a prop girl. From there, she'll get to know Thornton Wilder, and open as a member of the cast of mourners in the funeral scene of *Our Town* on Broadway. She'll take modern dance classes at Martha Graham's studio, and go to the city library to check out books, and to the Metropolitan Museum to see paintings, and she'll work as a file clerk at AT&T, where her boss becomes one of her dearest friends and, eventually, my godmother.

In the evenings, she'll serve Campbell's new brand of soup— cream of tomato—in city markets, little cups of hot soup that she'll offer to people, and there are many, who are hungry. And she falls in love with a White Russian, a member of a compound of exiles in upstate New York who'd fled the revolution. Although she spoke of him rarely, and then somewhat obliquely, I sensed he was the love of her life.

I love him, too, because he flies his plane down to the city to be with her. When he dies in a crash on a trip back to the compound, she returns to the playhouse on the Cape, works all summer and into early fall in props and costumes.

Back in the City, as it's turning cold, she will sign up for winter writing courses at The New School, where a tall, skinny student in the fiction class offers her a piece of chewing gum. She turns him down, of course. Chewing gum? When my father told that story, it made my sister and me laugh. He was from a prominent old Wisconsin family, come to New York to be a writer, and he found her beauty both compelling and intimidating. He thought chewing gum might make her smile—the absurdity of it—and it did.

In the hurried leave-taking and confusion of my college graduation, I lost my mother's map. She never quite forgave me for it. I hadn't taken seriously a time when the life she was searching for was all ahead of her, and she went forth to meet it. Without a way ahead for myself, I couldn't even begin to learn from hers. But the loss rendered the map indelible, its shape and markings scrawled forever in my mind along with my mother's story.

When my own journey did begin, that eighteen-year-old girl hiking the Cape threw me a lifeline. It took a while, but she led me to Thoreau, another lifeline, and I began to find my way. Before long, I had become a part of the back-to-the-land movement, starting a career as a writer and living in the woods on the coast of Maine, half a mile from the ocean. This place has given me some truths I choose to live by.

Thoreau's stories that feel like home to me are the Penobscot River trip he took with Joe Polis, the revered river guide, whose wit and cleverness equaled, and sometimes bested, that of the famous man he guided, and Thoreau's ascent up Katahdin, where he discovered what seemed to him to be the place where the Earth was born. It almost knocked him flat. On the Cape he faced the momentous fact of death within the everyday moments of our lives. On Katahdin he faced the gorgeous but terrible vision of vast time.

For my mother, it was *Walden* that gave her the start to make of herself what she wanted to be, and it was *Cape Cod*, the book and the place, that gave her the courage and the setting as the world slid into the Great Depression. You could call it a long meditative walk, a retreat from everything she had known before, a break so that she could begin to reach for something different.

My mother walks and the days pass, one after another, like a line of buoyant clouds across the sky. She crosses over from the bay side to the open ocean, and hikes along the high bluff, where she sees the colors in the bogs and the water out across the ocean, and the shadows down the sand's steep perpendiculars. They flare and subside, purple, green, blue, mustard, russet brown. As Thoreau did before her, she knocks at the door of the keeper's house at Highland Light in Truro on a late afternoon. He directs her down the beach to the Coast Guard building, where she knocks again, and the men on duty let her in. I like to imagine that they all turn at once to see her framed in the early evening light as if she had appeared out of a fairy tale—a rugged Snow White with a rucksack on her back—to transform, however briefly, the tedium of their watch. They contemplate her crisp radiance, her astonishing innocence. She comes to them with the sun going down, its long amber light resting against the water, and they receive her with utmost courtesy, and shyly, when she asks, they tell her they have never heard of Henry David Thoreau of Concord.

I believe, especially in times of change and trouble, we reach for the stories that we tell ourselves, and we tell them to each other. They remind us where we're from. Sometimes, they help us understand where we're going.

After supper, my mother said, the guardsmen offered her a bed in a little room to herself. There she wakes past midnight to the sounds of a storm, the surf devouring the base of the high dunes, the wind flinging sand against the windows, and the foghorn at Highland Light like the muffled hoot of an owl. Awake in the dark, staring out the salt-encrusted panes of glass to the huge candlepower of the lighthouse pulsing across the miles of water, she watches it circle and beam. Circle and beam.

FORERUNNERS

TWENTY-TWO

THE FIRST YEARS

WHEN YOU MOVE TO a new place, everything you see makes it feel as if it had been here just as it is now, forever. You have arrived and will be changed by it, but it is complete and immutable.

That is what I thought of Prospect Harbor when I first moved to the village with my family. I stared at this fiercely cold northern water, at the enormous flocks of winter eiders floating in undulating rafts upon it, the spare landscape—the granite extrusions, horizontal, the spruces around them, vertical—and the working harbor with the people who, as I listened to them, spoke in an accent that probably had more to do with villagers in a small, rural place in Britain three hundred years ago than now. It was the same language, of course, but the emphases were different, the pronunciations unlike my own, and I loved it.

We were lucky because we'd often be invited for tea by two women who lived down at the harbor in a wonderful old house. We took our children along because these generous women loved children, and we ate biscuits with jam and drank tea with milk and sugar, and they told us stories about the life here.

On the wall of the parlor where we sat hung a framed photograph of Marsden Hartley: the eyes as pale as a malamute's, the look wary, private, and also, I thought, passionate. He had kept company with them in his last years, and often visited the house, and sat in the parlor where we were sitting. They told us that Kate and Forrest Young had rented him a room in their home in Corea, a short drive down the peninsula, from 1940 until he died, in 1943. But other than some rather general things, they were circumspect in what they offered to tell us. Hartley could be a difficult man, and I suspect their affection for him kept them protective.

I found a book of his paintings at the Dorcus Library in the village, and checked it out a number of times. I wanted to see what this painter saw of the place where I lived. I found that he had rented the old Baptist church in Corea as a studio, and in the evenings, I had seen the fading crimson-pink sunset spreading from the west to the harbor water and reflecting in those gorgeous windows, in that completely silent chalk-white church. It was incomparably beautiful and lonely. He painted the church a few times, and in one canvas, it was as I saw it in the sunset, with just a slight tilt to the left, so that it became both an object of emotional transcendence, standing alone on barren ground in the oncoming night, and also a bit like a child's sketch.

I began to see this place I had come to through the imagination of an artist who had lived here, and it helped me understand that I wasn't just anywhere. I was somewhere.

Although he was long gone, the afterglow of Hartley's presence hadn't faded. He painted the church, and the rocks and the pitching water at Schoodic, the waves a heavy frothing blast of white. The mackerel that my son caught were the same as those in Hartley's *Sea Window—Tinker Mackerel*, the fish laid out on a red table by the window with a view of the bay and the islands beyond. I saw that his clouds, shaped like baking potatoes or icebergs, or strange, deepwater jellyfish, were perfect. They looked just like the clouds I saw. And the painting of the window giving to firs and spruces, with a path between them leading out to the bay I had seen from my neighbors' windows.

My children and I were learning about this place that was their first home, a world of seals and sea urchins and tides. Everyone I knew in Prospect Harbor and Corea worked hard and took risks. Those were the years of pretty good fishing, good boats without a lot of gear, a fair amount of money to be made on the water, and a coastal culture that brought with it a sense of pride and a way of speaking and thinking that was full of detail and ironic humor, some violence, some restraint.

But all this was already disappearing. And the water was getting fished out. We just didn't know it.

For my family, what Marsden Hartley had painted made this place as enduring for us as those smooth granite ledges we crawled over to get to Corea beach and to the curve of cobbled shore that led to a low-tide island. What we hadn't grasped yet, but were starting to understand, was that things change.

Things change. And although Hartley's paintings still described the world of these harbor villages, time was darkening it.

In 1940, he painted a still life of a common eider, its head to the left, its wings folded tight against its body, one foot held to the side. The bird is a male in full breeding plumage. It could be a duck shot last fall or a perfect thousand-year-old mummy dug up from an ancient tomb in the Corea Heath. You really can't tell which. We don't have common eiders rafting in this bay where I live now anymore because, for a number of reasons, we've lost most of our blue mussel beds, and mussels are their preferred food. But along the peninsula, in the spots where the mussels still grow thick against the rocks, these big ducks still gather.

The painting, which hangs in the Museum of Fine Arts in Boston, Hartley named *Black Duck*. (He grew up in the river town of Lewiston, without eiders, which are exclusively sea ducks.) The title doesn't matter. The painting does. It stays with you because he has honored, in death, the loveliness and the force of an individual life.

When I saw it at the Colby College exhibit of his work three years ago, it awakened in me images of our first years on the coast and of Hartley, the man with the malamute eyes, whom I had imagined had shared those years with us, and who had made them, for a time, timeless.

TWENTY-THREE

THE GIFT OF BIRDS

JOHN JAMES AUDUBON'S double-elephant folio, *Birds of America,* rests in its honored place in the Bowdoin College Library. Every month someone is invited to turn a page of these water-colored engravings, and in May 2019, I was asked to turn the page to the ruffed grouse. It is a ceremony I was, at first, honored to accept, although I had no idea what a double-elephant folio was, so I looked it up.

It's a book of the largest sheets of paper that could be put through a press in the early to mid-19th century, at 26½ by 39 inches. The folios were printed between 1827 and 1838 in Scotland and England, and the complete set is in four volumes. Only a hundred and twenty sets exist today, and the last time one was sold, in 2018, it went for $9.65 million.

The folio includes 435 hand-colored prints of 489 species of American birds. Audubon sought to create a book of prints as close to the size of the birds as possible, and although most species of birds are small, such as the wood warblers and the thrushes, many, like the American turkey, the trumpeter swan, the golden eagle, the great blue heron, and the turkey vulture, are large. He got as close as he could to the accurate size. What he seemed to want was to give his viewers the birds themselves, alive, right off the page.

As May grew closer, I began to worry. I was about to touch one of the most valuable books in the world. What if something went wrong? The worry presented itself, inconveniently, at night, in the dark, in bed. I saw myself holding the corner of the page between my thumb and forefinger, and turning it a bit hastily, I ripped the corner off. What if I sneezed (the old pages might be a touch moldy, and I am allergic to mold), and a spray of drops rained down on the irreplaceable prints as everyone looked on? And then there was the one where, approaching the folio, I tripped and fell on top of it.

During the day I was fine, but as the sun set, I started to think I should call to leave a message letting the staff at special collections know that I was suddenly, inconveniently sick. I knew that Audubon had left a summer's worth of work, about 200 drawings, in a wooden trunk in a Kentucky cabin once, and found, at his return, that pack rats had shredded the paper to make nests. Proof, it seemed to me, that anything can happen.

But my time at Bowdoin was a success. I lifted the page and lowered it to the two male grouse stretching their necks up toward a small cluster of ripe grapes that dangle above them, their tails and wings and ruffs in elegant color and pattern. Before them a watchful third stands in subdued buff plumage. What intrigues me about this event other than the kind staff and their devotion to the folio was that members of the public came to see the page turning and to listen to what I had to say about Audubon and his work. There's a lot to say about John James Audubon. I don't remember what I told them that day, but I do remember the huge page and its weight, and the solemnity of turning it. The people, about twenty-five of them, gathered close. It felt like a time not only to honor an indefatigable genius, but to honor our love of birds and the place they hold in our own lives.

John J. Audubon was a failure at the business ventures he started in America—except, of course, for one. He borrowed money he didn't repay; he lost interest in the work at hand and let it slide. Once he took a sizable loan from the brother of the poet John Keats, who had moved to Kentucky and met Audubon there. The poet later wrote, "Mr. Audubon (is) a dishonest man." But he was good at giving art lessons to children of prosperous families, and good at drawing their portraits for a fee and teaching them parlor dancing. He wanted to be out with wild birds, in the wildest parts of the unsettled eastern frontier that he could find.

He could be a charmer. A rather gorgeous and extravagant figure with long, flowing hair and buckskin fringes, he cultivated an image that seemed to many who met him in urban settings a throwback to a simpler, better time. He was also a man who held grudges against those who criticized his work because of his lack of scientific and artistic training—but who can blame him? He was reaching for something beyond what they required.

As a boy, born in Haiti to a French father in 1785 before the uprising, and raised in France, he was self-made in America. With a somewhat shadowy family history, he came into this new country, which gave him—and so many others like him—the opportunity to recast and invent who he was. It was an aspirational country for those of European descent, and Audubon had the energy and the brilliance and the subterfuge to make something of himself in it. He arrived when he was eighteen, when the land was still wild, although much of it had already been damaged.

He turned himself into a frontiersman as the Eastern frontier was dying. He was a storyteller. His narratives were full of the adventure and violence of the time and veered easily into fiction. What's absolutely true is that he was a painter of astonishing talent. And he chose birds as his subject and his muse.

He loved wild birds. He noted, in precise detail, how different species walk, fly, and perch, how they stalk their prey, build their nests, and raise their young. Even when young, and growing up in France, he was consumed with their beauty. Over time, he became proficient, and painted them in watercolors and oils. He drew thousands of sketches of them in different poses, and when he was putting together his folios, he kept an eye on the work of the engravers in Britain who turned the paintings into plates, and he took pains to ensure the accuracy of the colors in the prints. After years of work, he succeeded in becoming in his lifetime *the* famous American painter of birds. It took energy, endurance, a capacity for lasting affection, but he could be cruel. Once he took a boat down the Mississippi River, accompanied by two slaves from the family home to help him navigate. When he reached New Orleans, he sold both the boat and the men who had traveled with him.

He went everywhere: Maine, Nova Scotia, Newfoundland, Labrador, the Everglades, the Louisiana swamps, the Blueridge Mountain forests, as far west as the Dakota territory, and more. At camp in the wilderness, he brought with him hired gunners and he shot birds himself. He wrote home that the heap of dead birds beside his drawing table was the size of a hayrick. Another time he mentioned that if he hadn't shot a hundred birds in a day, it wasn't a good day.

There were no cameras until 1888. He couldn't draw a wild bird by sitting at the shore or at the edge of a cliff and watching it. The work he gave himself required looking at every feather, at the precise color and curve of the beak, the bare scales of the legs and feet. He sought a variety of individuals of each species: birds in molt, in breeding or first-year plumage, males and female, etc. But for us, looking back, it's difficult to connect his love to this easy killing.

The truth is, he liked to shoot birds. He shot lots and lots of them. And he wasn't above depicting an injured bird as it died. In his portrait of the black-backed gull taken from life, its injury is mortal, its suffering, visible. The white and black of the gull's feathers and the red pooling blood, set like a painting out of the Baroque, dramatically bring light up against dark. It's gorgeous and awful.

And yet, when you read what Audubon has to say about black backs, or as he has called them, the tyrant gulls, you find how much attention he paid them. As he toggles between recounting their predatory nature and the charm and beauty of the individual birds, you see that he's put himself right into their world. He knows them in a way that good science can't always reach.

I believe we need to take a long look at Audubon's art and read his journals and descriptions of the birds he painted because we are at a time in which we are doing a lot of looking back to see who we are by how we've behaved. It is not an easy task to get to know this man in full but knowing the part of our history that is his history may help us into the future. For a start, this brilliant, contradictory artist is familiar: He takes much because everything seems to be his for the taking. Yet, he wrote this: *A true conservationist is a man who knows that the world is not given by his fathers but borrowed from his children.* Did he borrow too much from us? Perhaps.

Rereading his journals, I see that he was appalled by the plunder wrought by his fellow countrymen in this new world—this wild paradise: robins shot during fall migration and piled shoulder high in Louisiana food markets, the torture of wolves, the killing of shorebirds on a massive scale.

In 1810, before Audubon became our premier painter of birds, Alexander Wilson walked into the failing general store in Louisville, Kentucky, that Audubon owned with a partner who did most of the work. That day was somewhat unusual because Audubon was behind the counter, and Wilson introduced himself. He was a Scotsman who, like Audubon, had become an American citizen, and through disciplined study and helpful mentors who were scientists had learned how to draw and paint American birds and to identify and describe species and make books out of his work. He came into the store with his finished books, looking for subscribers who would pledge money for those he was to write in the future, and the birds he was to draw and paint to complete this exhaustive task.

He spread his books on the counter, and Audubon got a good look at them, and decided not to subscribe, but instead, to take him out shooting and introduce him to bird species Wilson had not yet seen.

Wilson's was the first cataloguing and thorough description of the birds of North America. His paintings are somewhat like an excellent bird guide, posed, rather than the dynamic portraits of live creatures that Audubon eventually created. Unaware of what he'd sparked in Audubon, Wilson moved on. But from that day forward, Audubon took his art and his narratives of bird life more seriously and began to see himself not as a failed businessman, but as a successful artist and naturalist.

Out in the field, he worked at his table he set up by the tents, or in houses or inns where he rented rooms for himself and his gunners. His days were spent watching birds, shooting them, drawing and painting them, and, often, eating them for dinner. He had to get the eyes down first, before that wet glow of life died, and then he rigged up scaffolding and hung the bodies by strings, like puppets, so he could construct a tableau to imitate life. He was a man who searched for, and required, the dramatic, and his bird portraits remind some people of people more than birds—perhaps out of a scene from Shakespeare. But others disagree. They insist that posed birds are boring birds, and that Audubon was different, and better, because he put them smack into their complicated lives, often in the act of killing or being killed. He made them noisy, even though we hear nothing. He made them muscular and agile. He gave them to us as fellow travelers.

There are others who point out that he posed a number of the birds awkwardly, in ways their bodies don't naturally go when they're alive, which is probably due to attaching them to the structures he built after they'd died. In a few of the canvases and prints he makes mistakes. For instance, his painting of a rattlesnake attacking a mockingbird nest in a tree is horrifying, but rattlesnakes don't climb trees; rat snakes do. Nonetheless, art critics have called Audubon's folio the greatest picture book ever printed. It's more than that. It's what we inherit as proof of our country's lost splendor and abundance.

I still remember the faces of the people as we gathered together at the library around the portrait of the three ruffed grouse. I could feel their fascination as they looked at what was in front of us, and I knew then that Audubon reaches easily across time, because this is our story as well as his.

Frank Graham, Jr. in his book, *The Audubon Ark*, writes that naming an organization formed to preserve geese, pelicans, herons, and others after the painter who killed so many seems at first glaringly contrary. And he goes on: "But Audubon's idea of a bird, of birdness itself, passed into the nation's consciousness and influenced the way Americans look at the natural world. They see the physical organism, composed of feathers, bone, and flesh, of course, but even the drabbest plumages seems simply a sheath for that something wild and inexpressible with which Audubon infused his birds. Watchers utterly innocent of ornithology often feel this primitive emotional pull. Audubon, through his paintings, passed on a way of seeing to later generations of Americans and implied that in learning about birds, they might also open themselves to the poetry of their lives."

A way of seeing. The poetry of their lives. I choose to read the meaning of Graham's last sentence as the poetry of the lives of birds meeting the capacity for poetry within ourselves.

TWENTY-FOUR

INTO WILDNESS

I. THE ART OF SAUNTERING

HENRY DAVID THOREAU'S great essay "Walking" was published in the Atlantic Magazine in 1862. He defined his walking as sauntering. I used to walk, and that seemed fine to me, but now, under his guidance, I'm teaching myself to saunter.

What's the difference? When I walked, I concentrated on speed, on pace. I'd go over what I had to do that day. But I saunter and pause. I look around and listen. I give time for what might happen next. It's a long, slow thank you for the day ahead.

Thoreau writes that the word *saunter* might originate with those who took pilgrimages to the holy land, the sainted land: Sainte Terre. Or, he continues, it might spring from the idea of being without land ownership—*sans terre*—which, for him meant having no particular home but being "equally at home everywhere. . . . This is the secret," he announces, "of successful sauntering." Never mind that the word derives from neither of these roots, I saunter as if I had come home to landscape after a long time away and everything here has a holy shimmer.

On my first deliberate attempt to saunter, it was mid-July, and I walked a little less than two miles to the osprey nest at Patten Bay and back. The female was firmly planted in her nest, tending the young, and the male came soaring in with a good-sized fish—alewife sized—and carried it into the bowl of the nest, did some snaps and twists with its beak, as if opening a can of beans, then left. The female took over the fileting and serving, the young so small I could just about see the tops of their downy heads. On the way back, I found a pair of carrion beetles mating along the shoulder of the road, and came to a gully filled with swamp candles, their yellow flowers blooming with summer light; then a right turn up the hill past the cemetery where crow fledglings flapped among the gravestones, squawking for food. I remembered that the master saunterer wrote, "All good things are wild and free."

He warns us not to saunter when the day is nearly done, for you've already missed the best part. In late summer start early, when the dew's wet and chilly, and head down a narrow trail. The one across the road from my house, for instance, leads to a cove. If it's low tide, wading birds are beginning to fly in from the north. Their sharp calls sound like pure distance, as if they've already come and gone and their voices are mere echoes. If the tide's high, in the rules of the saunter, there's always time to jump in.

I am dedicated to this odd art taught by this odd man because I want to hold close the wildness left in my town. I want to know the details of native lives and land. The trick, according to Thoreau, is not to take your inside life out, but to go present and empty, and things will come. An eagle flies over a field of goldenrod, perhaps, or a red-bellied snake rests on the warmth of the tarred road (gently, you pick it up and set it into the bordering field), or the sun filters through the dancing leaves of a maple. Everything counts.

"Walking" is the essay in which Thoreau wrote, "In wildness is the preservation of the world." He meant not only the wild in the land, but what's left of the wild in ourselves. If we saunter out to meet wildness, it may show us exactly who and where we are and keep us whole in a broken time.

II.

I've read Henry David Thoreau's account of his July 1857 trip with Joe Polis on the Allagash and the East Branch of the Penobscot at least three times, and this month, I picked it up again. I have an old Apollo Edition of *The Maine Woods*, and each time, with a yellow highlighter, or a pencil, or a pen, I check the parts I especially love. The pages are covered with marks and comments, as if I'd traveled alongside Polis and Thoreau, although I would not have fit into that small canoe, nor survived the carry into Chamberlain Lake. The tote road, according to Thoreau, was most likely made by muskrats and finished off by hurricanes.

Two men of different histories and cultural persuasions on a trip together is an American fictional trope: Huck and Jim, Queequeg and Ishmael, Natty Bumppo and Chingachgook. This, however, is different. First, it's true. Second, it's a window into the closing of the 19th-century northeastern frontier. And, finally, it probes the sensibilities of men who are part of our country's history: Henry David Thoreau, a white man from the village of Concord, Massachusetts, and Joe Polis, a Penobscot from Indian Island. They are both very good at what they do—one an unparalleled writer, botanizer, and philosopher, whom E.B. White, with great affection, called "a regular hair shirt of a man," and the other famously at ease in the woods and on the rivers and lakes. He knew how to read them, both the big parts and the small details.

Thank god there is nothing politically correct in Thoreau's approach to the trip or to his guide. He writes what he thinks of Joe Polis and of himself, no matter how raw. To sentimentalize Polis would be to patronize him, a man of wit, self-respect, and curiosity about the world—much like Thoreau himself. Both men had endured periods of sharp suffering in their lives. Both were funny, ironic, and testy, and they pick at each other a bit: Polis finds Thoreau somewhat dense and repetitive. Thoreau finds Polis's stories rather pointless.

There is a point, at the start of the journey, when they are traveling by coach up along the river, away from Bangor, that Thoreau reports, without any attempt to editorialize, an exchange between a white man and Polis. He lets it stand as is. The white man announced that he wanted to smoke and turned to Polis demanding to know if he'd brought along his pipe. Polis was silent at first, ignoring what was really not so much a request as an order to turn over his pipe, and then, when pressed, said no. No one else in the coach said a word, knowing what was clearly playing out before them: A white man was free to take an Indian's pipe. And the Indian was required to hand it over. But Polis refused to put himself in that position. Suddenly, the reader sees how isolated Polis is in that cramped conveyance, and how brave.

We can look back at this journey and find two independent and principled people on a canoe trip who arrive at a certain level of understanding in a troubled country that was struggling to understand itself. Thoreau, at forty, had already spent his night in jail rather than pay taxes to a government that legalized slavery; he had spent two years in his cabin at Walden, and written about it, and in two years hence he would argue, passionately, for an appreciation of John Brown's failed rebellion. Forty-eight-year-old Joe Polis had represented his people in Augusta and in Washington. He was a leader and teacher who fought to keep open a grammar school on Indian Island because he believed in learning how to negotiate the ways of the dominant culture without losing one's own. He set a standard of excellence in a dark time.

Many of us know that Thoreau's last words as he lay dying were, "Moose. Indian." I like to believe he was reliving his time with Joe

Polis, maybe even paddling with him, as a moose stepped out from the trees to the river's edge.

On this East Branch trip, we meet not only loggers sawing away at giant white pines, but, Joe Polis, a man for whom wildness is comfortable, is home. Thoreau believed that even as we keep house in a village, as both he and Polis did, we need some unspoiled land beyond it—crepuscular and damp, or bathed with astonishing brightness, full of silence and sudden sounds, a great big place of danger and promise. And we need the people who know how to value it.

TWENTY-FIVE

A SNEEZE

A WEEK AGO, I drove through North Brooklin, past the farm-house that was E.B. White's home, and I decided that in this season of hope for a new year I will reread the book about Wilbur the pig; Fern, the girl; and Charlotte, the spider. I will take up their story once more because it never fails to offer a strong dose of what's decent and what's true—and right now we seem to be in need of both.

I drove past the barn where I like to imagine Fern and her brother Avery launching themselves out the open door on the rope swing, and where I like to imagine Wilbur living below in the warm manure pile. The force of the story of *Charlotte's Web* came back to me, its celebration of life in a barn, its wry humor, its moments of grief and courage, the clean simplicity of the writing that makes the whole thing ring sharp and clear like a brass bell.

When I taught writing workshops, I would often assign this book. It is very close to a perfect book—if there is such a thing— and we'd get to work figuring out some of the elements that make it so. Death is steeped into its pages, as is life, immediate, brightly colorful and witty, playing itself out against that darker back-ground. The counterpoint between the two gives White a chance to write some of his most moving prose about the beauty and joy of being alive. The book gives him a platform to explore the delicacies and strengths of a good friendship, and to present a cameo of the travail that can beset a writer as Charlotte begins her task of saving Wilbur's life by writing "Some Pig" in her web.

I read the book to my daughter when she was five. As we neared the end, I explained that although we were coming to a hard part, there would be a happy place soon after. I had my arm around her and began the page about Charlotte dying, and Wilbur demanding that Templeton cut down her egg sack so that he can carry it back to the barn in his mouth. Suddenly my voice wobbled and tears spurted out of my eyes as my startled daughter watched and waited. What was this?

Other mothers have told me similar stories. We prepare our kids because we love them and don't want them hurt, and then briefly, before we can collect ourselves, we fall to pieces. It's not that White planned to make us weep. Well, maybe he did. Maybe he was weeping himself. But I think rather it's that he has trusted us, his readers, with such tenderness. It's that gift of trust that makes us weep.

White wasn't fond of questions about how he came to write the book. They seemed beside the point to him and a bit nosey. Once someone in the publicity department of his publishing house asked him just such a question, and he answered, "Three of Charlotte's granddaughters are trapping at the foot of the stairs in my barn cellar, where the morning light, coming through the east windows, illuminates their embroidery. . . . I haven't told you why I wrote the book, but I haven't told you why I sneeze, either. A book is a sneeze."

He's right. It starts as a tickle you can't get rid of. It builds up pressure and you feel that pressure growing until you can't think of anything else. And then—at last—a vigorous, satisfying "ACHOO!" In 1952 *Charlotte's Web* came into the world with its inspired illustrations by Garth Williams, and it's been with us ever since.

Some Sneeze.

TWENTY-SIX

LEARNING TO SPEAK

MY GRANDSON IS ELEVEN MONTHS OLD and the sounds he is making have changed. They aren't words quite yet, but there's a familiar cadence to them now, a rhythm that mimics the language he hears around him. I listen to his preverbal declarations, and it occurs to me that this is an essential moment in the emotional and cultural life of a child: we, the older generations, are seeding this particular language in him, with all it carries, which he will one day speak.

A writer is always listening to the sounds of a language as well as for the sense of it. Before I knew I was a writer, my father often read to me in the evenings—back from his commute to the city and after he'd poured himself a stiff bourbon. He chose for me what his mother had chosen for him when he was a young boy, had contracted tb, and the doctor's orders had kept him in bed for two years. During that time, his mother, who was English, read to him the poems she loved: Gray's *Elegy Written in a Country Churchyard*, Arnold's *Dover Beach* and *The Forsaken Merman*, Wordsworth's *The World Is Too Much with Us*. As a child, I was listening to this sober stuff as my father had done, but I was also getting the sounds and beat of the language set into memory: *The sea is calm tonight. The tide is full. The moon lies fair upon the straits* . . . etc. Those evenings, and the high church Sunday services, with their King James translations, were where I began to learn what the language I spoke could do.

Language connects people to each other, helps them identify who they are, and gives them a way to explain the world and their place in it. It also connects people to their landscape. Words originated to describe and interpret where we live, and as the world changes, the language carries that formative DNA into the new.

What if you were told that these words you carry, and the way you've learned to frame your thoughts with them, were valueless, that they were, in fact, a shameful connection to a defeated and impoverished people? That's what happened here in Maine, in Wabanaki schools, when Wayne Newell was a child on the Sipayik Reservation at Passamaquoddy Bay.

At first Newell didn't attend the reservation school run by nuns because he was legally blind. Instead, he was kept at home, where his parents and their relatives and friends spoke Passamaquoddy all day long—a last generation that spoke the language whole—and it was the depth and constancy of that language, disparaged by the dominant culture, that were his first lessons in defining the world around him. As his contemporaries in the schoolyard were taught to abandon their first language for English, his early life was steeped in it. His mother and grandmother saw no reason for him to enter a schoolhouse as a young blind child. Rather, he was treated to stories told by his elders of what it means to be Passamaquoddy, and they sought to teach him to distinguish between the poverty they struggled against and the culture they celebrated.

When I got to know Wayne, I asked him if he would tell me more of his story, how he got from being the blind boy at home to a spokesman for his tribe and a conservator and teacher of the value of the language that belongs to his people. He began by telling me that in 1949, when he was seven years old, a cataract surgeon in Portland unwrapped the postoperative bandages from his eyes. He opened his right eye—the left one had never worked—and the world was different. For the first time he saw more than fuzzy shapes and shadows. "My God, everything was so clean!"

After that operation, he got lonely staying home while the other kids left for school. One day, he walked into a classroom and sat down. He didn't want to be left out anymore.

Today the Penobscot and Passamaquoddy tribes in this state not only have created school programs to teach their own languages, but have honed the language of the dominant culture to define for themselves who they are to the larger community, and to describe what their history has been for them, and what they believe their responsibilities are as First People on this land. In part, this confidence comes out of the 1980s Land Claims Settlement Act, an imperfect document, but one that gave them, and the Houlton Band of Maliseets, a voice, though not the clear and independent agency they hoped for. Another is the work the Penobscot tribe, alongside a number of organizations, has done to clean up their river. And it comes out of the years of resurrecting the original languages and teaching them to their children. Wayne was at the heart of that reconnection, what you might call a tribal operation to restore vision. He was one of the first to build and direct a bilingual education program in the Indian townships.

Over the years I have visited Wayne, and we've talked about his life and his thoughts, and I've called occasionally—sometimes just to check on how he's doing. He's become an elder himself now, having given his best thoughts and energy and years to his people. The younger generation speaks for the tribe today.

What I find remarkable about Wayne is his good humor and his insistence on framing his path through the world as one of opportunity. How many people would find it a promising prospect to start out life as a legally blind boy in a small, remote, exceedingly poor Indian reservation, as it was back then? All those years ago, with almost no resources, it looks like a recipe for a difficult, self-defeating life, but for Wayne, it seems to have been the start of a bildungsroman: young boy sets out to make his way in the world.

"I've always been lucky. I've been at the right place at the right time." When he saw that I was startled by this declaration, he explained that the pediatric cataract surgery that gave him sight, for instance, was a brand new technique back then. Also, the year he walked in and sat down in the reservation school, it had just begun receiving books in large print, as well as records and tapes he could listen to. In high school, he flunked his sophomore year, repeating the grade the next fall. But the second time around, he won first prize in a public-speaking competition, and that was enough to plant in his mind the idea that he might move in the direction of making a public life for himself.

He left the reservation and enrolled and then dropped out of two colleges. It looked briefly as if his life might have stalled. When he returned home, without a degree or prospects, he was hired as a cameraman at a local Bangor TV station. "I was probably the only legally blind TV cameraman in the whole country," he tells me.

That TV station was another "right place at the right time" for him. It's where he first heard John Stevens, the Passamaquoddy governor, speak to a broad audience. Stevens wasn't a gifted speaker. It sounded to Wayne as if he were translating too directly from the Passamaquoddy of his youth into English. The presentation was halting, somewhat stilted, but the content inspired Wayne. Stevens was a smart, principled man who argued pointedly for Indian rights.

Wayne watched, he listened, and then decided to turn his life around. In the next year he won a Ford Fellowship for leadership development and went to Washington, D.C. as an intern in the Economic Development Administration. There he learned about ways to help his community back home. In his spare time, he volunteered in Ed Muskie's office. He married, came back to Maine, and was told by Ed Hinkley, a friend of his, as well as the state commissioner of Indian Affairs, that he should apply for a master's degree at the Harvard School of Education, in a program that was recruiting community organizers.

He laughed out loud. "Ed," he said, "I don't have a bachelor's degree—and you want me to apply to graduate school at Harvard?"

Hinkley countered, "Make a case for life experience."

That night Newell sat down and wrote about his life and his hopes for his people. The next morning, he sent the pages off, and was invited by return mail to Cambridge for an interview.

What follows is a story I treasure because it speaks to the difficulties negotiating both culture and class, and to Wayne's buoyant humor. Here he was, about to go to an interview at one of the most prestigious universities in the world. What does he do? He drives to Bangor and buys a dark blue suit and a tie to go with it.

"I said to myself—Harvard—I can't go looking like a bum. I bought that beautiful suit, thinking this is how they want me to look."

Newell arrives on campus during the height of the demonstrations against the Vietnam War. He crosses the Yard where the police had cleared demonstrators the night before, and walks to the interview room and opens the door. Before him sits a group of white men around a long rectangular table. "They've got beards," Wayne says, "and they're wearing flannel shirts and jeans. Oh, my God! I'm standing in front of them dressed like an undertaker!" He roars with laughter at the memory.

Harvard accepted him into the program, and he moved to Cambridge with his wife and child in 1970. He was a man with a dream, and tireless. Before long he'd cross-registered at Massachusetts Institute of Technology and was deep into studying the problems of turning an oral language into written form with the renowned linguist Kenneth Hale, who studied the oral languages of the Americas. Wayne also worked with another famous linguist,

Karl V. Teeter, who had already tried transcribing Passamaquoddy. Newell wanted to build on that beginning, and Teeter told him, "Go right ahead."

When he returned to Maine, Wayne was hired to run a demonstration program in bilingual education at Peter Dana Point in the Passamaquoddy Township at Big Lake. The old days of nuns and the prohibitions against first languages were over, and he worked to include Passamaquoddy in every classroom. Since that time, he never let up: he directed the language and culture program at Passamaquoddy schools, helped set up a health clinic on the reservation, served as president of the wild blueberry company owned by the tribe and on the University of Maine's Board of Trustees. But the achievement he is proudest of today is the 2009 publication of The Passamaquoddy–Maliseet Dictionary: *Peskotomuhkati Wolastoqewi Laltuwewakon*. Both David A. Francis, also Passamaquoddy, and Robert M. Leavitt, professor emeritus at the University of New Brunswick, worked alongside him.

"Newell deserves the lion's share of the credit," Leavitt told me. "He initiated and oversaw both the Passamaquoddy dictionary project and the creation of recordings, books, and teaching materials based on traditional storytelling, music, and oral history."

Wayne says that he kept in mind this question: What would help future generations continue learning and speaking the language? "If we didn't get more people speaking fluently again, we wouldn't have teachers for the next generation."

One of the most precious things he owns is a tape of an original recording on a wax cylinder, made in 1889 in the nearby coastal city of Calais. It was the first Native American language recording ever made in this country. He told me that he imagines five or six Passamaquoddies, men and women, gathered in a room somewhere in that city, sitting on hard-backed chairs, leaning forward and speaking into the horn of the machine for a traveling ethnographer, their soft, vowel-studded voices barely audible. If he could have reached across the years to ask them, what would they have told him they hoped for? Perhaps they'd say that 135 years later, they hoped that their people would still be here.

Wayne believes, and I imagine that this tape recording has influenced his belief, that if you have to study who you are by using a language that belongs to another culture, the intimacy is lost. To experience the depth and breadth of your own culture, you can't really learn about it in another culture's language. And at the same time, he says, education was the great liberator for him and for others on the reservation. And that education came to him in English. He was keeping his balance by standing with a foot in both languages, both cultures. At ten years old he had learned enough English to be a passionate reader, but he never gave up his Passamaquoddy.

What do we know of the inside of a culture by looking at it from the outside? And what keeps people alive during generations of crisis? I drive by the brick homes at the side of Big Lake at Peter Dana Point today, and most of the signs of the old derelict shacks are gone. Trauma takes generations to heal, but here at Indian Township is the reservation center with its dramatic cemetery overlooking the lake, the health clinic, and the tribe's ample, well-equipped school and sports fields. I remember driving by in the '70s, stunned by the poverty, and I've learned since then that looking from the outside never gets you far. What appears to be terminally broken may have within it some deep, abiding fires of regeneration. As it did here.

Language carries within it a sense of time, a sense of being a people living in a certain place, with a particular history. All this is embedded in the words that are made out of experience and passed on through generations.

When I think of Wayne, the picture I hold is of him sitting by the plate glass window of his living room that looks out at Big Lake, vast and shimmering in the light of high summer, and he's got his head cocked to one side as he listens again to the tape of the voices from long ago. They belong to those half-dozen people who walked into a room and sat down to speak to the future in a language they didn't want forgotten.

THE LIVES
OF BIRDS

TWENTY-SEVEN

HOME ON THE RANGE

WITHIN THESE WOODS OF tall white pines, firs, spruces, some oaks and red maples, my house sits in a small clearing, a bright round bowl full of sunlight. The casement windows face south.

I spend more time than I like to admit looking out them, drinking tea, pondering a paragraph or a chapter I'm working on, and because it is very quiet here, I see things: an ermine snatching up a vole from its snow tunnel; a doe shouldering through the heavy drifts to get to the apple tree; a bobcat a-doze in the herb garden in high summer.

One of my favorites things to watch begins as a line of dark shapes in the woods moving toward the clearing. At first view, it's a shadowy ghost march back in the dusk of the trees. But as they break into the light, they become glossy, beautiful birds. Our neighborhood's wild turkeys.

Four toms—for some reason it's been four in full breeding regalia most springs—gather in the clearing with slow, dramatic tail fanning and staccato wing dragging. They're rough jousters, but they also perform a bit of synchronized dancing in twos, stepping forward together in high display. The females mill about them. Then, one after another, a hen prostrates herself on the ground, inviting a male to clamber onto her back. Which he does, too awkwardly, it seems to me.

Eventually the mating season ends, and they disappear, except for one, a shy female who creeps out of the woods at high noon for a dust bath in the garden before she tiptoes to her nest again. I always hope that, whoever she is, she'll present her offspring, marching them across the field so I can see them.

Three hens brought their mixed brood of fifteen into the clearing last summer. The young, who were about two weeks old, swarmed awkwardly over everything as the hens uttered cautionary clucks. It was an especially hot afternoon, and the poults must have been wrung out from a day of swarming, because the three dams took them to a bed of dry sphagnum, and the little ones plopped down at their feet and fell fast asleep. Just like that. Some with their wings spread wide. Some folded, with their heads tucked in their shoulder feathers. The hens stood guard, figures of stern vigilance, as I stood at the window with my cup of tea.

Best of all they returned at dusk, and did so for a number of nights, as I watched first the hens take off running, spread their wings out, beat them furiously and lift up into the high branches of the pines, more than thirty feet above the ground. Then the little ones started, by twos and threes, popping into the air and heading straight toward their mothers, until there was one left. With the windows open I could hear its frantic peeping and the guttural sounds of the hens that seemed to be coaxing it on, until it took a brave chance and flew. Then all was quiet, and all night they slept on branches right outside my bedroom windows, and at dawn, I found them up in the pines just beginning to stir.

It has taken years of work for biologists to bring back the peregrine falcon, the bald eagle, the wild turkey. These birds occasionally grace my landscape now, returned to a changed environment that once belonged all to them. And they make changes to what they find here.

They are the gifts from the people who don't want to lose what's wild, and they are proof that we, who have made deep incursions into the lives of others, sometimes choose to fix what's broken.

TWENTY-EIGHT

TO CATCH THE
MORNING SUN

SOMETIMES BIRDS WE THINK of as belonging somewhere else—birds from away—increase their range northward year after year and become one of our own. What brings them here? It may be a warming climate or changes to their habitat or to their food supply. Sometimes they follow roads that open up easy pathways, like rivers do.

Once a bird of the south, the turkey vultures are part of our seasonal fauna now, like the thrushes that arrive in April, and the hummingbirds that come back looking for last summer's feeders around Mother's Day. In March, these vultures ride the thermals above our roads, moving northward in slow, circling migrations. In a day, they can coast in a widening gyre from Massachusetts into Maine.

Following roads north in the spring is a good idea for vultures. That's when mammals and birds are on the move, which means that some are killed by cars, and turkey vultures are the age-old cleanup crew.

Ora Knight's *Birds of Maine*, published in 1906, records a handful of turkey vultures in the state in summer. By the '70s, though still somewhat unusual, more were taking the thermals north. The '70s is when I came to Maine. I didn't see them then. They kept to the southern part of the state in the summer and retreated in the fall. But in 1982, the first turkey vulture nest was discovered on Camden Hills. And now, you're as likely to see them in early spring, drifting above the roads in Down East Maine, as you are to hear a robin's song.

Like them, I had come here to make a good life. While I learned to knead bread and plant seedlings and raise two kids, they were raising their young in hollow logs, on ledges, or in forgotten sheds and under abandoned cabins. Silent, except for an occasional hiss or muted growl that you'd hear up close when they're disturbed or excited, they are sober and serious about the work they do, which is to make festering corpses found along our roads and in our fields and woods disappear. One of the few species of bird in the world that has not only exceptional vision, but a superb sense of smell, they can detect carrion a mile away.

If you hold up the skull of a turkey vulture to the light, one of the things you notice first is that the nostrils are big and open. You can see right through them from one side to the other, and the olfactory lobes, within the skull, are the largest among New World vultures.

This may seem a passing detail, but in the world of ornithological dustups, the question of how New World vultures find their prey has been an issue of dispute ever since John J. Audubon decisively and incorrectly proved that turkey vultures can't smell, that they find carcasses by sight. One of the most interesting clues to their unusual ability to hone in on a scent came when a Union Oil worker, in the 1950s, mentioned to a researcher that the company had added a rather rotten scent to its oil in order to locate leaks in the overland pipes, and the workers learned to key on circling turkey vultures overhead to pinpoint the leaks.

Now we know that turkey vultures, taking to the thermals, are reading the world below with their noses, as well as their eyes, and black vultures, without much of a sense of smell at all, follow them, just as the Union Oil workers did.

Some years ago, driving down a dirt road to a Costa Rican wild-life sanctuary along the Nicoya Peninsula in the evening, my son and I saw at a distance over a stretch of savannah a large tree and beneath it a half circle of at least ten black birds, standing as if they were monks at a ceremony. As we got closer, we could see the body of a dead cow, and as we drove, a coyote crossed the road ahead of us, heading toward the monks. What we didn't know then, and do now, is that turkey vultures, which these birds were, must wait for another species, such as a coyote, to pierce the hide of the dead.

Their beaks, as white as pearls, can plunge into pliant places. Eye sockets, anuses, an open mouth. But the odd thing about those beaks is that although they look like formidable cutlery, they are not good at ripping through the tough hide of large mammals like deer or cows. The birds stand around, having snacked on the softest parts, and await either the bacterial volcano inside the corpse to stretch the skin and cause suppurating leaks or for someone else to do the initial opening. Birds such as ravens can often pierce the tough skin, but they also devour as much flesh as they can manage as the turkey vultures, who are not particularly aggressive, wait their turn. This seems unfair, when you consider that the turkey vultures, with their acute sense of smell, have done the work of setting the table and presenting the feast.

❦

Last week I was sitting on a wooden chair in the corner of a 15-by-10-foot flight cage, roofed, with welded wire fencing on three sides and wooden boards on the fourth. The floor is dirt, rocks and sticks strewn across it, and in the center rested a hard rubber watering pan.

Anne Rivers, who runs Acadia Wildlife, a sanctuary for wild animals where the mews is tucked beside the main building, had handed me the chair and let me in. I was grateful to her, because I'd come to see this bird whose home this is. Before me, up on a plywood platform, stood a male turkey vulture in adult plumage. He was poised behind a dead tree trunk and peered at me from one side of it in a posture of hesitant curiosity, his head cocked. One gleaming obsidian eye checked me out. An unreleasable bird, he lives here, and I was sitting in his parlor at the edge of his safe place.

While other species of birds might show signs of panic at this abrupt intrusion, he didn't. Turkey vultures are social. They enjoy company. I spoke a few words to him, softly, and he responded with a step out from behind the tree, and a bit of pacing across the plywood toward me and back, his toenails clicking on the board, some fluffing up and some more head cocking, but nothing to indicate that he was frightened—curious, obviously, a bit unsure, yes, but no outright fear.

Turkey vultures can live thirty years, and he looks healthy, gleaming, in fact. The odd thing is, to me he appeared at first more like a person than a bird, a man out of the 16th century with a jet black collared ruff around his neck, a serious fellow, and well educated, perhaps in the process of translating the Bible from Greek into English with a sharp quill pen; or he's a warden in the Tower of London during Henry VIII's reign, when the wardens wore wide ruffs around their necks and guarded unlucky queens. He didn't seem to be of this time or place. He was too formal, somehow, and the way he strutted back and forth on the plywood stage looked like he was contemplating something deeper than I can guess about the world we find ourselves in.

Above the neat ruff rose his red, wrinkled neck. His head, also red, and mostly bare except for a few tufts here and there, comprised the gorgeous dark eyes and the hard, white nail of his beak. His legs are gray. His feet have startlingly long thin toes, like a heron's. His wings—a 5½-foot span—were folded thickly at his sides.

I had been told by Anne that he is smart and social, has warmed to his handlers, and enjoys a bit of play. He wears jesses on his legs because he eagerly steps onto a falconer's glove when offered for a hike around the wildlife center (the jesses clip to a ring on the glove). However, if he were taken into a classroom and held on the glove for children to enjoy, he might grow uneasy in such a new place, with too many people staring at him and talking in too many voices. He might panic. A panicked turkey vulture goes quickly into self-defense mode, which is to spew a projectile splatter of vomit. Nothing smells as awful or is as acidic as turkey vulture vomit, an effective defense in the wild, but a game-changer in a classroom. Here, in his safe cage, he's the boss, gentle and elegant. A wonderful bird.

Nothing moves quite like a vulture. Out in the wild their dihedral flight means that they lift their wings in a slight V-shape, tilting gently from one side to the other, catching an upward draft on one wing and then on the other to take themselves forward or higher, as they please. Sometimes, they gather together and wheel across the sky in slow circles, flapping occasionally. Watching from below, it seems to me to be a restful way to be up there. On the ground these vultures stride and hop, and "lollop," a word I love, which means to bound heavily along.

Last summer a neighbor told me about some strange birds in a crawl space under an abandoned cabin. When I walked around it, I found a turkey vulture nest, which is no nest at all, just a hidden spot on bare ground, and shone my flashlight into it. Two puffs of brilliant white down feathers, as big as beach balls, scrambled backward, hissing. As a parent circled above, I leaned over and focused on the nestlings, white as milkweed fluff, with coal black heads and legs, their eyes glistening in the dark. I didn't stay, but the image of the two stays with me, especially now, as that cabin is tidied up and renovated for someone's summer house, someone other than a nesting bird.

Early this morning I walked up the Cross Road hill and along Morgan Bay Road to the place where a big field slopes down to the bay and the mountains of Acadia stand up in the distance, framing to the east this small town where I live. A thermal updraft rose off the water of the bay, moving steadily uphill. It was warm on my face, and the sun rose above the mountains and shone on the water, bright in the clear air. Suddenly, I noticed that the big oak by the side of the hill was filled with five turkey vultures perched on its strong branches, wings spread wide like heavy curtains opened to the sunrise.

TWENTY-NINE

GOING TO SEE THE DUCKS

I COULDN'T WALK THEM BLINDFOLDED, but I've followed the paths to the head of the bay near my house for years, and I could probably, blindfolded, tell you where we were if you stood me at almost any point. At least I like to think so.

In late fall, in winter and early spring, I take to the path up through the woods, then down the tidy steps to the eastern cove, or I cross a neighbor's field to the ledges. As the tide advances, rising against the layers of schist and lifting into the dead stalks of the Spartinas, the winter ducks are out along the bay. I'm not here to discover something new, but rather to see the ducks I think I know, and to be reassured by them that some important things still remain.

This past fall, as the days grew short, I waited for the buffle-heads and the goldeneyes, small and medium-sized black and white ducks, to return. We'd had a lot of bad news from every corner of the world, and if I'd been told then that these ebullient divers I was waiting for had taken off from their summer nesting ponds to the north and vanished into thin air, I might have believed it. And the winter would have been drained of an essential joy.

But they were there at last, on the cusp of serious cold, as busy and hungry and buoyant as ever.

The bottom at the head of the bay is shallow and muddy, with tangles of seaweeds and clumps of barnacles and periwinkles around the rocky edges, and in that bowl of water there are mud snails and worms, small arthropods, soft-shell clams, and the darting fish that the tide brings in. Winter ducks like this sort of food. They like the calmer water here, surrounded by a windbreak of tall trees.

Before they arrive, in late fall, when the shorebirds and the waders have passed through, except for a lingering great blue heron still stalking the low-tide edge, there are a few days when the water is as clean and empty of birds as a washed plate. And, also, in the heart of winter, when ice has sealed the head of the bay tight, no one else is out there except for a herring gull or two flying across, looking down to see what's in the cold fissures where the rising water pools.

Originally, buffleheads were named buffalo-heads, after the big-headed bison of the prairies, because the male's striking black and white head is large for such a little duck with such a delicate bill. It has a full feather crest that makes it seem even larger. It's the smallest diving duck in this country and weighs less than a pound with a wingspan of 22 inches. The people I knew who worked on the water in Prospect Harbor called these plump little birds butterballs.

Arthur C. Bent, the famed ornithologist who wrote *Life Histories of North American Birds,* called the bufflehead "charming" and gave it the name Spirit Duck. Ornithologists tend to rhapsodize over buffleheads not only because of the clean, dramatic beauty of the male, but the birds behave as if they are happy—playful, even. We, onshore, bundled in layers against the winter cold, watch as they frolic in that deadly water. Although they have an intertwining mesh of veins and arteries that warms their legs and feet, and they have layers of down more insulating than what we are wearing as we watch, they still seem a bit miraculous.

Bent, impressed with how buffleheads take off from the water, wrote that the legs of diving ducks are set farther back on their bodies than other duck species. Those legs don't just dog-paddle along but are used in a dive to swim after quick prey, escape danger, and barrel straight down to hunt stationary food at the bottom. They are more like the arms of an Olympic swimmer doing the butterfly. Legs that aren't centered on the body make it difficult for diving birds to rise quickly off the water. They have to pump their legs and beat their wings hard, tripping across the surface of the water at great speed to launch themselves. But buffleheads manage it. They can also pop up from a dive and head into the air as if it were one continual gesture. This may be due to their small size, and to the fact that they stay just above the water's surface as they fly.

Fishermen on this coast have always called the common goldeneyes the whistlers. If you stand at a winter shore where these ducks are rafting out on the water, you'll hear the whistle every time one of them takes off. It's a high whirring made by the wings. Bent calls this beautiful duck exceedingly wary and sagacious, due to its long history of being hunted. However, like the bufflehead, it is also playful out on the water within its winter flock. With brilliant white breasts and flanks and their dark heads that during breeding season glimmer with a blue-green tint, and with a bold white circular patch under each eye, the males posture and dive and bob to the surface again. The eyes of both the male and the gray- and rust-colored females are large and, no surprise, bright yellow.

I've never seen the goldeneyes and buffleheads in summer, but sometimes my imagination follows them along a green, shady course of a Canadian river, zigzagging around oxbows. I imagine a bufflehead hen flying along the banks of a remote taiga pond hunting for a tree with an empty and available nesting hole of a flicker, or a goldeneye hen searching for pileated woodpecker nesting holes. I've read that these ducks can squeeze themselves into spaces in trees that you can just about fit your hand through, sideways.

I hardly recognize them like this. They are more than I knew: freshwater birds, insect-, and pondweed-eating birds, tree-nesting, shy and secretive and fast.

Today, it is March fever out on the bay. No secrets here. Nothing shy going on out here. The male goldeneyes churn the water around the hens, gesticulating like mad court jesters. And the exquisite bufflehead males are dashing at each other, raising wakes in a frenzy of mating readiness, preparing for a trip to a place so unlike this bay.

Wild ducks—wild animals of all sorts—fire the human imagination. Where do they go from here? How do they behave when we no longer see them? We pursue them in our thoughts. In our dreams sometimes we invent what we image of their lives as our lives reach to embrace a wider, wilder understanding.

THIRTY

A HOMECOMING

I.

RESTORING A NATIVE SPECIES almost always introduces it back into an altered habitat. Biologists sometimes take that risk. They know that some species will adapt to the differences. Others may not. It's often difficult to predict which species will succeed and which will fail.

On a summer afternoon along the shore of this bay where I live, I sat down at about a hundred feet from the two bald eagles standing in the low tide on a ledge covered in seaweed. I lifted my binoculars to watch them. The top avian predators along this coast, they gaff fish by raking their talons through the water and dispatch a duck as if they were wringing out a wet towel. They're also good at kleptomania, as anyone knows who has watched them pressure an osprey to release the fish it's caught.

These eagles are a mated pair. They had an easy comradery as they poked around in the seaweed together, swishing their beaks in the still water of the bay, lifting their talons to clean them with those heavy beaks, fluffing up and sleeking down their feathers. When they unfurled and flew off, from wing tip to wing tip they cast two six-foot shadows across the water.

Bald eagles are a part of our everyday lives now. In the white pines by their nest at the shore, the fledged young and the adults talk together constantly, their voices thin, high, and sharp, as if they were small quarreling songbirds. Sometimes their calls are strident, whistling blasts, echoing over the water to the far shore.

An eagle will stop to peer down from its perch in an old pine on my land, checking out the bird feeders. It couldn't maneuver quickly and tightly enough around the trees to catch a chickadee or a nuthatch—and what would be the point of snatching up such a tiny nub of food, a body not much bigger than one of its toes? And I doubt it could catch a red squirrel—only because of the trees. But I could be wrong.

My town of Surry is thirty-seven square miles of land and almost fifteen square miles of water. That's a lot of edges on bays and ponds, where these birds like to live. The last eagle census taken here records five pairs nesting in Surry. We're smack in the center of eagle territory.

What might not be as clear is that we almost lost them in this state, in this country.

In 1981, Charlie Todd, a biologist with the Maine Inland Fisheries and Wildlife, along with Mark McCullough, a doctoral student in biology from the University of Maine, were given the task of restoring bald eagle numbers to the state.

With a mandate such as this, the first question becomes restoring to what time period? How many eagles can the land and water, which have changed over the last five hundred years, support?

Do we aim for a number that we estimate may have lived along our rivers and shores at the time before White Contact? Or before the beginnings of industry along the rivers—before we dammed them, preventing anadromous fish from reaching their spawning grounds, and before factory discharges polluted them? Or when mechanization just began to come to the woods, and lumbering, instead of a logging camp with men who worked with axes and saws, transformed itself into an industrial enterprise? Perhaps back to the time of the opening up of forests for pasture and farming, the cutting of trees along our saltwater bays and riverbanks, ponds and lakes, diminishing the abundant nesting sites of these birds and turning wild stretches of coast into pastural townships.

As this landscape was settled by people of European ancestry, we attempted to eliminate, as best we could, wild predators, including wolves and some raptor species, such as eagles. In the 1930s, when Arthur Cleveland Bent was compiling *Life Histories of North American Birds*, he carried forward this commonly accepted view of the bald eagle: "Its carrion-feeding habits, its timid and cowardly behavior, and its predatory attacks on the smaller and weaker osprey hardly inspire respect and certainly do not exemplify the best of American character." It isn't that he's describing the bird's behavior incorrectly, he's not. But he's requiring a wild bird to carry human traits—cowardly? timid?—and a sense of moral rectitude, which we don't carry particularly well ourselves.

The writer Henry Beston called species that are not our own "other nations." While I am not convinced that the concept of nationhood to describe them is a good one, it's true that wild species have evolved techniques all their own over long stretches of time to be good at what they do—find food, find a mate, stay alive—which has nothing to do with the aspirational values of a human construct of country.

Bent added in his monograph on the eagle that in Alaska bounties were set on the bird in 1917, and for the next ten years they were paid out for 42,000 kills. A few towns along this coast, where townspeople traditionally kept sheep on islands, also instituted bounties into the early 20th century.

DDT entered the food chain in 1939. It killed birds, such as the American robin, by poisoning the food they ate. Bald eagles and ospreys began to lay fragile eggs that broke in their nests, because the chemical, which they ingested by eating fish, closed down their bodies' ability to use calcium. Outlawed in 1972, thanks to the brave work of Rachel Carson, DDT is no longer legally in use in this country, Canada, or Mexico.

And, finally, we know a lot about the demise of our fisheries because we have the numbers and the losses at hand over years of records from state and federal agencies and from the fishing community itself. So why work to bring a fish-eating, big-tree-nesting, apex predator back into a depleted environment?

The answer has a lot to do with the birds themselves. They are primarily fish eating, that's true, but they are also generalists. They'll pick up a fish or a duck, a house cat or a farmer's chicken or a dead raccoon on the roadside, and they're supreme opportunists capable of hunting for food, or stealing it, over a wide area.

Mark McCullough remembers watching eagles when winter ice had closed off large areas of Cobscook and Frenchman Bay. He saw the birds hovering and dropping down to ducks that were swimming in a little spot of open water in the middle of the ice-up. The ducks would dive to get away, and then come to the surface, and the eagles would drop down again until the ducks were totally exhausted. Then the eagles would pluck them up.

This state began an effort to clean up some of the toxins in our rivers in 1972, and in 1999, the Edwards Dam was taken down on the Kennebec River. That historic—and heroic—gesture of freeing a river opened the way for other dam removals in the state, along with town-sponsored endeavors to install fish passages along local streams where there once had been plentiful fish runs. And the fish came back.

"Now alewives, shad, and eels—all sorts of migrating fish—are in abundance. They are what eagles used to rely on," McCullough says.

These migrating fish, returning to spawn (or, in the case of the American eel, moving to the sea to reach its spawning ground) present a seasonal bounty. Today, as in the historic past, the fish that go from salt to fresh water run in numbers great enough to fill up the river channels. Eagles descend to the spring feast. But these brief migrations end, and the rivers flow freely again, and the fish are gone.

The efforts to address river waters that caused disease in people and fish and birds, and opening up rivers and streams to fish migration, along with the prohibition of DDT, were all hopeful signs that as bald eagle numbers began to grow, as the state and the nation worked to restore them, our stewardship of their former habitats would continue to improve to welcome them back.

However, out in the bays along the coast, fish species that don't migrate into fresh water to spawn and that do swim close to the surface where eagles can reach them, such as Atlantic herring, are slow to come back to their former numbers.

When Mark McCullough was given the job of restoring bald eagle numbers, he began in Washington and Hancock counties, where the residual numbers of the birds were the greatest. It was a seat-of-the-pants operation. He had made a trip to Nova Scotia to visit a farmer who was putting out on his field cattle that had died, and eagles learned to key on that food source. The farmer liked the birds, liked helping them out, and McCullough thought he and Todd could replicate that feeding-station approach here during the winter months to keep the birds alive through the hardest time of the year.

As he looks back at those first years of stocking Down East winter-feeding stations with clean carrion for the birds, he says that a primary issue was to be sure that what he set out in open fields contained no lead shot. The smallest fragment from a hunter's bullet can poison an eagle and kill it.

He was accepting a surprising number of donated cow and horse carcasses from farmers, an occasional moose, and a large number of roadkills. Eagles, like turkey vultures, do not have beaks that are chisel shaped. They need ravens to pierce the tough skin of a large carcass, or they need the sharp canine teeth of a coyote to open them up. McCullough took on that role himself, opening the dead with a double-bladed axe so that the birds could easily reach the flesh and entrails. Then, covered in gore, he'd scoot under a tarp thrown over a picnic table, focus his scope through a hole in the tarp, and observe the birds as they fed. If he was lucky, he could make out the numbers on the leg bands that researchers had put on the eagles when they were still in the nests. Those numbers told him where they had fledged and when.

As he recounts these years of work, he laughs ruefully. No one had thought of doing anything like this before. It was messy and low tech, but over time mature and juvenile eagle numbers at the winter-feeding stations began to grow. He identified them as pairs from local nests, and some juveniles from as far away as Michigan and Saskatchewan.

"We documented that maybe close to a third of our young eagles stay in Maine for their first winter. They came to this source of food we put out. Others drifted southward, as far as Chesapeake Bay. They aren't migrants. They're drifters looking for open water.

"In summer, we banded and radio tagged the young eagles. We found that they followed their parents around the nesting territory. We never, in all our years of observing the pairs and their young, saw the parents show the young how to feed on their own, never saw a young eagle attempt to catch its food. They got a hundred percent of it given to them until the parents grew tired of doing this—and left. Then the young had to figure it out. We learned that for them finding and killing to survive is instinctual, not learned."

One event in the years of work, he says, left him with some regret. He was brought a living horse, old and beloved by its owner. As the owner held the reins, McCullough was asked to shoot it in the forehead, where the vet had indicated was the precise point to kill the animal fast and without pain. McCullough had become used to opening up the dead, but to be asked to kill a gentle old horse was more than he was up to. However, reluctantly, he eventually did it. The horse dropped and the owner left.

It was a hot October afternoon, McCullough told me. He stripped to the waist and began the task of opening up the body. Suddenly, a voice came from behind him. He turned, covered in the horse's blood and holding the double-bladed axe, to find the owner asking him for the horse's bridle as a keepsake.

Winter food, clean food without lead bullets, the return of some fisheries, and strict fines for shooting a protected species all contributed to bringing the eagle population roaring back.

This basic and bloody restoration plan achieved more than imagined. When it began, only about thirty to sixty pairs of eagles nested in Maine. Today their numbers are now close to eight hundred nesting pairs, and that doesn't count the immatures. Bald eagles take four years to mature to breeding readiness. The young birds that stay here all year and those that come back in the summer, according to McCullough, may number as many as a thousand.

The bald eagle was removed from the national list of Threatened and Endangered Species on August 9, 2007. In Maine, it was delisted in 2009, although the species is still given protections under other authorized acts, both federal and state.

II.

If there's one thing that Maine people treasure above all else, and I am not sure there is just one, it may be the beauty, isolation, and wildness of its inner and outer islands, some close to shore, others far out in the Gulf of Maine.

In the spring, species of seabirds come to some of these islands to nest. Among them are black-backed and herring gulls, Arctic and common terns, Atlantic puffins, razor-billed auks, common and thick-billed murres, black guillemots, Leach's storm petrels, common eider ducks, double-crested and great cormorants.

On the islands closest to shore great blue herons used to nest in the tops of trees, grouped together in heronries. Their nests look like bad hair days, but they are surprisingly sturdy, and the young, as they grow, poke their long necks up out of the nests, waiting impatiently for a parent to return and throw up a meal. Bald eagles have damaged these island heronries, and the herons have abandoned them to seek nesting sites inland.

"When we were flying eagle surveys back in the early 1980s there were some islands on the coast that were big colonies of breeding herons but they are no more," McCullough tells me. "That's largely because of the eagles. They'd move right into the middle of the heronry, even taking a heron nest and building it up to make it their own. Then they'd pluck up the little herons in the nests nearby and it doesn't take long before the herons say, 'we're utta here.' It's one species that's really changed because of the eagles."

Species of seabirds that nest on islands farther offshore are colonial as well. They come to the islands that have often been used by them for generations. There were years of market hunting, egg gathering, and shooting the birds for the feather trade, but that unfortunate history is done, and the islands, set apart from the

mainland, are chosen by seabird species for their protective isolation and distance from the mainland.

The populations of seabird nesting islands has rebounded, but
these birds are vulnerable due, in part, to rising water temperatures
that can result in changes in fish species that the birds depend on
to feed their young, and to predation by the occasional owl and
falcon. Biologists and state and federal agencies over decades have
worked to protect them, to ensure, as best they can, that they will
return to the islands and the young will fledge. Some field biologists
have made their careers working for the well-being of our island
nesting birds.

Bald eagles have always taken seabirds and a wide variety of
ducks, even at times when fish were plentiful. But now, with the
surge in eagle numbers and the drop in inshore fisheries, a number
of the nesting islands have become scenes of pillage, with eagles
perched on rocks, waiting to snatch up a young unguarded cormorant, an eider hen, a herring gull chick, a puffin flying in with a
beak full of sand lance to feed its young. It's a tapas bar for the big
birds, and inevitably, for some in the scientific community, the joy
in their resurgence has turned to alarm.

Five years ago, as predations increased, Richard Podolsky, an
ornithologist and a former research director for the Island Institute,
wrote an article entitled "A Once Rare Bird Now Eats Another." He
was responding to reports of eagle depredations on great cormorant
nesting islands.

Steve Kress's inspirational work to restore Atlantic puffins to the
Gulf of Maine through years of patience, an abundance of hope,
and a number of creative techniques eventually brought the birds
back to their former nesting islands. He believes that it's worth the
effort to protect the cormorants now: "bringing them back if they

were to disappear will be a much more difficult process." Eagles, he writes "are a great success story and part of a larger good news story about big predators. . . . On the seabird nesting islands managed by the Audubon Society, we found that the presence of resident 'seabird stewards' makes all the difference. It's all about timing and people moving around the islands. On Seal Island National Wildlife Refuge, a team arrived about two weeks later than usual one year and found an eagle pair building a nest on an observation platform. The birds abandoned it when they saw humans. It shows how people can help, year by year, to address the issue—but it's not a 'fix.'"

Brad Allen, bird group leader for Maine Inland Fisheries and Wildlife, tells me there are probably fewer than forty pairs of great cormorants nesting on Seal Island today.

"It's frustrating," he says. "We can't kill the eagles, of course. Great cormorants are at the southern boundary of their range in the Gulf of Maine. They were extirpated before, so we want to keep them here if we can. But we're on the edge of it happening again. The U.S. Fish and Wildlife had put interns out on Seal Island earlier in the spring and kept them there later in the fall than they used to stay to dissuade the eagles from disrupting the cormorant colony. Other than that, we're at a loss as to how to deal with it."

I called Mark McCullough to ask him if, with successful fish runs in the rivers and perhaps eventually a growing number of fish in our bays, he thinks that the eagles might ease up on seabirds out on the islands into the future.

"No. I don't think they will," he says. "I think they're honing in on the birds. The migrating fish are available for a couple of weeks—but the eagles have to eat the rest of the year, and there are many more eagles than there have been. That pressure is going to be there."

III.

Dan Jansen, an evolutionary ecologist renowned for his work on the dry forest of Guanacaste, in Costa Rica, chose to focus on restoring habitat, not species, more than forty years ago. It was a new concept. He picked a precise time in the forest's history before farming and mining and cattle ranching, and then meticulously researched the native plants that grew at that time. He couldn't have done it without the support of the Costa Rican government, which paid miners and farmers to convert themselves into researchers and caretakers and wardens of the land and helped him hire young biologists to join in his fieldwork. The Costa Rican government under President Oscar Arias figured out a way for ranchers to do their work outside, rather than within, the designated conservation area of the Guanacaste. Over the years, which were full of promise and inevitable failures, the land slowly became various and native again. When it could sustain species that were endemic, they returned on their own. Gradually.

Another story that gives me hope in the promise of habitat restoration is the work at Cabo Pulmo on the Baja Peninsula in Mexico. That small fishing community had lost their fishery due to overharvesting. With the help of the Mexican government and field scientists, they organized a commons around its fishing area in the Sea of Cortez, prohibiting all fishing for ten years, except for a limited area where local people were allowed to fish for their sustenance, but not for market.

The community, with the help it needed available, built for themselves the rules they would follow, and the fishermen took on jobs such as monitoring the borders of the commons, working with field scientists, and taking tourists out in their boats to show them what had happened to the bay and how they were working to repair it. After ten years, the sea commons was not only replenished with local wildlife, but people from all over the world came to experience this startling resurgence of reef, coral, fish, and other underwater species and habitats.

It was decided by the community, the government, and the scientists that maintaining this area as a model of what the inshore life along Baja used to look like, and could look like again with work and vigilant care, was too important to let it slip away into old habits of overharvest. As a result, they made it into a conserved park, run, in part, by members of the town. There is pressure to open it up to fishing again—there always will be—yet the boundaries have held, and the area has become, over the years, even richer, more diverse.

That's the "build it and they will come" approach. It differs from the work of inserting an endemic species back into a changed habitat and waiting to find out what happens next. Instead, it reestablishes large areas of former habitat to a point of health; then people who did the restoration work wait to see who comes. Both approaches have risks. Now, in Maine, we are scrambling to figure out how to protect osprey chicks, great blue heron chicks, great cormorant chicks, eider ducks, and more.

Individual eagles are dying unnecessary and painful deaths from the continued use of lead shot, but as a species they are doing just fine. Forty years ago, no one would have believed it. We are putting back together some healthy habitats in this state, imperfectly, too slowly, and piece by piece. It's worked for the big birds, although they've taught us that we need to do much more to protect the birds they like to eat.

This is the future: species at the edge have a chance if we choose to attend to what they need before they start to slip away. Sometimes they require something big: a clean river; fish in the bays; wild seaweed beds growing, uncut, along a protected shoreline; a stable climate. Other times, it's opening a dead cow with a double-bladed axe, or hiring a young intern to spend her summer on an island to protect the birds she will come to know and, perhaps, to love.

Kayaking at the end of summer on Toddy Pond in the early morning, I passed an eagle's nest built halfway up a white pine. Next to it stood a bird of the year, full grown, upright, dark chocolate brown. It was an emphatic being, fragile and fierce at once.

THIRTY-ONE

AT DUSK

BY THE ROAD WHERE I LIVE, in an open field in front of the bay and the woods beyond, April wakes up the land. Last evening, neighbors and I gathered with camp chairs on a driveway across from the field that borders salt water and watched the light seep slowly from the sky and clouds close in as we listened to the last sounds of daylight: a robin's song, a few shouts from the herring gulls heading out to the islands, and a tom turkey's faraway gobble. Then a span of silence before the peepers started up their ringing calls within the alders down the road.

We had come for the spring song and dance of the woodcock. We sat, or stood, our ears sorting out the crepuscular noises, waiting for the peculiar sound of this bird, one of spring's most tonic wake-ups.

When I lived in Prospect Harbor with my kids and former husband, I heard a woodcock's voice for the first time. The call is a "peent." If you say it in a low register while holding your nose, you're pretty close to how the bird says it. But it's even more like some sort of bizarre electrical malfunction.

One night, the first spring we lived at the coast in our cabin back in the woods, I woke up, in the middle of a dream, to the full moon and an alarming sound.

"Robert," I whispered, shaking him awake. "The wires to the cabin have broken!"

"Wires to the cabin?" he mumbled, still half asleep.

"Electric wires. They're making a buzzy snapping sound."

He was quiet for a moment. We both were. And it came again: Peent.

"But we don't have electricity," he said.

"Oh, right! Of course! What is it then?"

"I have no idea."

We both got up and tiptoed into the kitchen. Through the big window to the south we watched, by moonlight, the strangest thing: a football-shaped bird doing a sort of shuffle on the ground and uttering that most unbirdlike sound.

On this year's April evening a couple brought along their grand-daughters, eight and five years old, happy girls, excited to be out at dusk. Another neighbor walked slowly up the small rise to the driveway to join us and eased himself down into a chair, somewhat distanced from the rest. I was thinking as I watched him that we'd come to this field so many times that this had become as much a celebration of ourselves witnessing another spring as it was about welcoming woodcocks back. I saw that he had turned frail over the winter, and when the girls played around him, he was especially delighted and gentle with them.

The first time that neighbors and I gathered at this field, years ago, we sat along the trunk of a downed tree, opened a bottle of Jameson whiskey, and passed it back and forth as we listened to the woodcock. When the light fell away and the bird stopped singing, we walked home along the road, our flashlights bobbing in the cold, spring dark.

As the male woodcock began his show last night, we, sitting or standing in the driveway, heard the first peent—whispered faintly— at the far end of the field. It grew louder, more authoritative as the bird swung into action. After a number of preparatory peents, he took off into the ebbing light, a speck spiraling up into the sky, higher and higher, the twitter of the wings sounding like something sweet and mechanical, faster and faster, until the bird had climbed to a pinnacle that he alone determined was far enough, well beyond where we could see with the clouds closing in. A rapid chirping told us that he kept his place in the sky as if it were a toehold on a mountain crag before he slanted sideways at great speed, emitting sweeter chirps as he slashed through the air, landing, unbelievably, just where he began, and peented again.

Woodcocks, chunky birds, cautious and secretive by nature, become these hugely dramatic performers during the mating season, when the male throws himself into his complicated flights, and mates with any female who is drawn to the territory he claims. One year, I came alone to this field early in the season and watched two males duke it out for possession of the territory, the strangest guttural noises coming from them both as they hurled themselves horizontally in each other's direction. As far as I could tell, they never touched.

There's not much about this shorebird that is what we think of as shorebird behavior. The bird isn't the flocking sort that gathers with others of its species at the tide line and flies away with them in perfect synchrony as if they were one. No. It carries on a solitary life. Keeping to the edges of the woods and within alder patches, it hunts worms and beetle larvae and such. It's the color of old leaves and mud and the shadows thrown by the branches of the overhead trees.

We know how shorebirds run, light footed, sometimes bobbing up and down charmingly from tail to head. The woodcock, a Minister of Silly Walks, jolts its body forward and back like a rusty porch swing: Forward and back. Take a step. Forward and back. Take another.

For years, ornithologists argued about whether the music of the male woodcock's flight came from the wings or the bill. Turns out, it's both: first the wing-twitter, then the voice-chirp. Some birders of old insisted that female woodcocks carry their young from one place to another between their legs, until it was clear that they don't. But it's probably true that when they patter their feet on the ground as they feed, the soft drumming mimics rain, encouraging earthworms to move up toward the surface. The bird's strong bill, which is exceptionally long compared to the size of its body, has a sensitive, pliant tip full of nerve endings. The tip of the upper mandible lifts underground like an index finger to catch and hold a worm.

It's not much of a surprise, since most of the things about this bird are already a surprise, to learn that its brain has been somewhat rearranged. The cerebellum sits at the base of the skull. This adjustment accommodates large eyes located near the top and toward the rear of its head, as opposed to each side of the head, like robins' eyes, or straight ahead, like the eyes of owls and hawks. The placement allows woodcocks to probe vigorously deep in the dirt as they keep a lookout for predators.

For those of us who gathered here last night, it was all about honoring life in springtime—ours and everyone else's of varying species that live here all year or have just returned—although none of us said a word. This is a wonderful place to be alive in. We'd made it through another winter, and our reward was to be by this field, to listen to the bird's call and his flight starting up again—and again.

At last I picked up my chair and walked back to the car past the head of the bay, where a line of black ducks floated quietly on the water in the channel. They were beautiful to see, ghostly silhouettes in the fog and the oncoming dark, about thirty of them, all facing in the same direction. I knew that they would be stepping out onto the mudflat the channel runs through before the night was absolute, and in the last purplish light from the sky glinting off the mud, their dark shapes, moving like miniature buffaloes across a prairie, would be gleaning all that small life we don't often see.

Behind me I heard the children laughing and the man sitting in the chair laughed along with them as the woodcock again rose into the sky.

THIRTY-TWO

THE GULL

FOR A NUMBER OF YEARS, my parents rented a small gray-shingled cape on a dirt road close to the beach in the town of Dennis, on Cape Cod. We came for a month in summer. One August, when I was nine, they returned with my sister to Connecticut, and I stayed on with the Criders, New York City friends who had inherited a cottage that sat on a high dune facing Cape Cod Bay.

It was called a cottage, but it was a big, airy, echoing 19th-century house. Easily comfortable with itself and its legacy of summer children, it was dark inside, the floors and walls and ceilings built of wood that smelled of rubbed oil. The light reflected off the sand and the direct light of the sun entered through the windows and shone rectangles against the walls and the floor. Their daughter Sammy and I went from the beach to the house as we pleased. We rinsed our feet at the tap by the back door. We never wore shoes.

Outside, four other summer cottages had been built along the dunes, set apart from one another, each massive, and made of the same dark wood. Before them, the bay water curled and slapped, bringing in to the tide line all kinds and shapes of wild sea creatures. The wind blew, the beach stretched, glittering, beyond our sight. Few people ever came to walk or swim here, where Sammy and I climbed the wild dunes that were covered in sharp beach grass and rested in the warm pockets between them. Over all of this, the gulls screamed.

Sammy was a year younger than I. We wore boiled wool sweaters in the evenings, old sun-bleached shorts and one bathing suit after another during the day. This casual life was, of course, a childhood of privilege. We were unaware that we were the last generation of children to summer here in this timeless way, that the cottages would be swallowed up by development, driveways bulldozed into the dunes, the beach a draw for many, not just us. The cottage we lived in that summer was an assault on the wild, but it was a mild first guard, and what was to come vanquished the particular life it oversaw.

None of this crossed our minds. We were two blond girls, tan and freckled, skinny, strong, rather simple. The days went by. We ran along the edge of the tide collecting moon snails and skate egg cases and clumps of seaweed—splays of knotted wrack and dark purple Irish moss that dried in the sun to a brittle beige. We swam. At night we lay in our beds reading by lamplight. But there were times I drifted away from Sammy, went off down the beach until I could hardly make out the cottage. I lay down in the hot cups of the dunes alone, watching the grasshoppers and spiders that lived among them, and the patterns that the grasses drew when the wind blew them sideways and they spun like crazy clock hands.

That was how I found the gull.

It was walking along the line of seaweed and flotsam the waves had tossed up, poking at one thing and another with its yellow beak, and dragging a broken wing. For a while, I watched it, as I lay between the dunes. Then I got up and chased it down.

It sat quietly in my hands, its head pointed forward, one wing folded against my hand, the other, slack. I held it out in front of me, and all it did was pump its legs as I carried it back to the cottage. Deep into the dense feathers of its body, my fingers touched its heat and the quick pumping of its heart.

Sammy's parents had gone shopping in town. I found a cardboard box and set the gull in it, and Sammy helped me fashion a pen for it out of some old boards stacked around the back of the house, a broken beach chair, and a window screen. When we had finished, I lifted the bird into the pen and brought it fresh water and a hard-boiled egg I found in the refrigerator, two slices of bread, and half a sausage. Sammy and I sat on the back steps and watched the bird devour the food and take drinks of water, lifting its beak up to the sky so that the water would run down its throat.

It preened, poked at its hanging wing, and then stood still, its yellow eyes betraying nothing we could read. After a while, Sammy lost interest and wandered back to the beach for a swim. But I had touched the bird, felt its heat. I couldn't take my eyes from it.

When Sammy's parents returned, her father stepped from the car.

"What's this?" he said.

"I found it on the beach," I told him. "Its wing is broken." The bird had skittered sideways at the approach of the car, tripped on its wing, and righted itself.

"And this is a cage?"

"A pen," I said.

"A pen," he said.

Sammy's mother stood holding a bag of groceries in each arm. Her father smiled.

"Well," he said, "let's try this for a while. Let's see what happens."

Without a word, Sammy's mother carried the bags of groceries up the stairs and into the house.

Looking back, I can guess at Sammy's mother's disappointment. The girl who would keep her child company had gone rogue and built a ramshackle pen by the house to contain an injured wild animal. A week went by. "It smells," I heard her tell her husband in the kitchen one afternoon.

The gull bored Sammy. I left my vigil by the pen only to hunt for crabs and moon snails along the beach, which I smashed open with rocks and fed to the bird. Back and forth, from the beach to the pen, I was relentless, and the gull was hungry.

What drew me, what fascinated me, was its beauty and its remoteness. No matter how close I got, it was a wild life I was tending, and that wildness, I understood, was absolute. What hurt, what felt like a wound in myself, was the plain fact of the broken wing I had no power or ability to heal.

The days of summer were ending. The beach had a raw, sharp edge to it now, and sometimes, in the early morning, a hard wind cut down the whole length of it, and the water, beyond the beach, was gray and rough.

One day Sammy's mother came to sit beside me on the back steps. "You're leaving on the train tomorrow, Susie. I think it's time to put the gull back," she said.

"Where?" I asked.

"On the beach where it came from."

"But it can't fly."

"It will be fine," she said.

I looked straight into her face. "I don't think so," I said.

That evening, as the Criders gathered to play a board game together in the living room, I walked into the wide, dark hallway to call my mother on the wall phone.

I am familiar with the tone of voice she heard when she picked up the phone at our house in Connecticut. I have heard it from my own children on occasion. It's the voice that wants something so urgently and is afraid it won't be given.

I explained to her, as my voice echoed in that bare, high-ceilinged hallway, that she needed to drive back to Dennis tomorrow to pick me up because I had to bring a gull home in a cardboard box in the car.

"A what?"

"A gull."

"A bird?"

"Yes. It has a broken wing. Please, Mom."

I heard her clear her throat and get quiet as if she were thinking it over, as if, perhaps, she might think it made sense. Then she said, very gently, "The Criders are going to put you on the train tomorrow and you are not allowed to take pets onto the train with you."

"It's not a pet," I said.

"Bird, then," she said. "Wild bird. I am very sorry."

She waited patiently as I wept into the phone. The hallway amplified my grief, but I didn't care. I can only imagine the scene in the living room beyond, the Criders listening in a stunned silence.

That night I got out of my bed and tiptoed downstairs and sat on the back steps watching the gull sleep with its head turned into the feathers of its shoulder.

Sammy's father, whom I had seen on my way outside sitting in his favorite chair in the corner of the living room reading, came out and sat with me. He talked to me about the beach, and how every summer he couldn't wait to get here, and he asked what I thought school might be like this year, what grade I was entering, and if I knew who my teacher might be.

His job was in the executive department of the Bronx Zoo, and he told me how much he loved wild animals, and one of the best, he said, was a vulture with pale blue eyelids that was kept in a big cage with a ladder made out of tree branches for it to hop up onto a platform high enough so that it could see almost all the other animals in the zoo. He said it was a special treat to see it slowly blink its eyes. It was caught in Africa, he said. A long way from home, he added.

After a while, he got up, patted me on the back, and went to bed. I watched as the moon gave the cottage and the sleeping gull a thin dusting of silver. Then I went to bed, too.

The next morning, I carried the bird down the beach. It was stronger than before, and twisted its head around, but it didn't reach back to bite my arms. Again, it paddled its legs as if swimming. Its drooping wing, draped over my left arm, gave off a rush of feverish heat. And again, the fingers of my left hand felt its heartbeat.

From this distance I watch that child carry the bird into the gray dawn. What does she know? Almost nothing. She's brand new. But over the years, that injured gull on the beach has flowed into my life, into the land I live on now and the water and the wildlife I have come to love—this broken, beautiful place. I believe this happens to us all, a moment that seems to be one of many becomes caught in the amber of time, and it glows, and we can see by it something of who we were and who we have become.

I left the gull where I had found it and walked away. Only when I was a number of yards down the beach did I dare turn around. The gull stood, looking straight out at the bay, its beak a deep yellow, the white feathers of its belly lifting a little in the breeze, its legs pink, its feet webbed, its eye a harsh gold. Around it swept the broad curve of sand, above it the gray sky, and out where it set its gaze, the waves caught the muted light of day.

When we see land as a community to which we belong, we may begin to use it with love and respect.

—Aldo Leopold, 1949

ACKNOWLEDGMENTS

I THANK MICHAEL STEERE, my editor, for encouraging me to put together these stories that examine and celebrate aspects of what it is to make a home on the Maine coast, and working with me to make a book. I am indebted to Michelle Tesler, my agent, for her kind guidance and patience, and to Elaine McGarraugh, senior production editor at Rowman & Littlefield for her help and good eye. John Cornell gave me the gift of his photograph of the least sandpiper in flight close to shore. It carries, perfectly, the spirit of this book.

There are many people who have shared their expertise with me. Their knowledge and goodwill are at the heart of this work. I have to start with Aran Shetterly who has read many drafts, generously offering his time and talent; Maggie Budd Miller who critiqued the first essays and gave essential advice; Cynthia Thayer for her careful edits; and Kate Mrozicki for her read-through of the chapter on Wayne Newall. Brian Kevin, editor of *Down East* magazine invited me to a wonderful two and a half years of writing short essays for the magazine, a number of which I have expanded. They are included here.

Seth Bentz, Brad Allen, Bill Townsend, Rosemarie Seton, John Meader, and Diana Winn answered my questions on scientific issues; Mark McCullough, Sarah Redmond, Sandy Walczyk, and Gayle Kraus shared their science and their stories; and Wayne Newall told me stories of his remarkable life.

Paula Mrozicki and Susan Curran kept me going through some of the tough moments of putting a book together, and Margot Lee

Shetterly helped me whenever I asked. Hugh Curran sent me articles on subjects I was writing about, as did Charles Guilford.

I am especially grateful to the people of the Blue Hill Heritage Trust for the brave, skilled work they do protecting land on the Blue Hill Peninsula, for the work of the Downeast Institute to preserve fisheries and teach students about the ocean they live by, and to the people at the Downeast Salmon Federation who have worked tirelessly to bring back the health of streams and rivers on this part of the coast.

A number of the essays in this book began as "Room with a View" columns in *Down East* magazine. A version of a longer article, rewritten as "Learning to Speak," also first appeared in the magazine.

An early version of "The Gull" appeared in the *Sun*. "The Preserve" and "Becoming a Flock" first appeared in *Yankee* magazine.

ABOUT THE AUTHOR

Susan Hand Shetterly is the author of *Settled in the Wild* and *Seaweed Chronicles: A World at the Water's Edge*, as well as several children's books including *Shelterwood*, named an Outstanding Science Trade Book for Children by the Children's Book Council. Her writing has been longlisted for the PEN/E.O. Wilson Literary Science Award and shortlisted for the New England Society Book Awards. Shetterly has received a nonfiction writing grant from the National Endowment for the Arts, an Alfred P. Sloan grant, and two Maine Arts Fellowships. Recently, she contributed monthly essays to *Down East* magazine, some of which have been expanded and included in this book. She lives in Surry, Maine.